ASPEN PUBLISHERS

Friedman's
Practice Series

Contracts

Edited by

Professor Joel Wm. Friedman

Tulane University Law School
Jack M. Gordon Professor of Procedural Law & Jurisdiction

Wolters Kluwer
Law & Business

AUSTIN   BOSTON   CHICAGO   NEW YORK   THE NETHERLANDS

© 2007 Aspen Publishers (reprint of 2005 edition by Precedent Press).
All Rights Reserved.
http://lawschool.aspenpublishers.com

No part of this publication may be reproduced or transmitted in any form
or by any means, electronic or mechanical, including photocopy, recording,
or any information storage and retrieval system, without permission
in writing from the publisher. Requests for permission to make copies
of any part of this publication should be mailed to:

Aspen Publishers
Attn: Permissions Department
76 Ninth Avenue, 7th Floor
New York, NY   10011-5201

To contact Customer Care, e-mail customer.care@aspenpublishers.com,
call 1-800-234-1660, fax 1-800-901-9075, or mail correspondence to:

Aspen Publishers
Attn: Order Department
PO Box 990
Frederick, MD 21705

Printed in the United States of America.

1 2 3 4 5 6 7 8 9 0

ISBN 978-0-7355-7348-2

About Wolters Kluwer Law & Business

Wolters Kluwer Law & Business is a leading provider of research information and workflow solutions in key specialty areas. The strengths of the individual brands of Aspen Publishers, CCH, Kluwer Law International and Loislaw are aligned within Wolters Kluwer Law & Business to provide comprehensive, in-depth solutions and expert-authored content for the legal, professional and education markets.

CCH was founded in 1913 and has served more than four generations of business professionals and their clients. The CCH products in the Wolters Kluwer Law & Business group are highly regarded electronic and print resources for legal, securities, antitrust and trade regulation, government contracting, banking, pension, payroll, employment and labor, and healthcare reimbursement and compliance professionals.

Aspen Publishers is a leading information provider for attorneys, business professionals and law students. Written by preeminent authorities, Aspen products offer analytical and practical information in a range of specialty practice areas from securities law and intellectual property to mergers and acquisitions and pension/benefits. Aspen's trusted legal education resources provide professors and students with high-quality, up-to-date and effective resources for successful instruction and study in all areas of the law.

Kluwer Law International supplies the global business community with comprehensive English-language international legal information. Legal practitioners, corporate counsel and business executives around the world rely on the Kluwer Law International journals, loose-leafs, books and electronic products for authoritative information in many areas of international legal practice.

Loislaw is a premier provider of digitized legal content to small law firm practitioners of various specializations. Loislaw provides attorneys with the ability to quickly and efficiently find the necessary legal information they need, when and where they need it, by facilitating access to primary law as well as state-specific law, records, forms and treatises.

Wolters Kluwer Law & Business, a unit of Wolters Kluwer, is headquartered in New York and Riverwoods, Illinois. Wolters Kluwer is a leading multinational publisher and information services company.

CHECK OUT THESE OTHER GREAT TITLES:

Friedman's Practice Series
Outlining Is Important But PRACTICE MAKES PERFECT!

All Content Written By *Top Professors* • 100 Multiple Choice Questions • Comprehensive *Professor* Answers and Analysis for Multiple Choice Questions • *Real Law School* Essay Exams • Comprehensive *Professor* Answers for Essay Exams • Free Digital Version

Available titles in this series include:

Friedman's Civil Procedure

Friedman's Constitutional Law

Friedman's Contracts

Friedman's Criminal Law

Friedman's Criminal Procedure

Friedman's Property

Friedman's Torts

ASK FOR THEM AT YOUR LOCAL BOOKSTORE
IF UNAVAILABLE, PURCHASE ONLINE AT
HTTP://LAWSCHOOL.ASPENPUBLISHERS.COM

ABOUT THE EDITOR

Joel Wm. Friedman
Tulane Law School

Jack M. Gordon Professor of Procedural Law & Jurisdiction, Director of Technology

BS, 1972, Cornell University; JD, 1975, Yale University

Professor Joel Wm. Friedman, the Jack M. Gordon Professor of Procedural Law & Jurisdiction at Tulane Law School, is the lead author of two highly regarded casebooks -- "The Law of Civil Procedure: Cases and Materials" (published by Thomson/West) and "The Law of Employment Discrimination" (published by Foundation Press). His many law review articles have been published in, among others, the Cornell, Texas, Iowa, Tulane, Vanderbilt, and Washington & Lee Law Reviews.

Professor Friedman is an expert in computer assisted legal instruction who has lectured throughout the country on how law schools can integrate developing technologies into legal education. He is a past recipient of the Felix Frankfurter Teaching Award and the Sumpter Marks Award for Scholarly Achievement.

Table of Contents

CONTRACTS ESSAY EXAMS

QUESTIONS

CONTRACTS ESSAY EXAM #1

FACTS: JOHN ASHCROFT, THE EARLY YEARS

The current Attorney General of the United States, John Ashcroft, is rapidly developing a reputation as one of the grumpiest and most humorless men ever to hold the office. Though it would not have seemed possible during the term of his predecessor, Ashcroft makes Janet Reno look like Jay Leno. Until recently, no one knew the source of Ashcroft's generally foul disposition and demeanor. You are about to learn it.

It seems that, in 1998, during Bill Clinton's final term as President, Ashcroft became so disgusted with politics that he retired temporarily to a house on his ancestral farm in Fort Stinkinbog, Missouri, intending to make his living off the land. The farm, which Ashcroft had inherited from his father years before, was a 100-acre tract suitable primarily for grazing cattle. It was known locally as "Ashcroft Acres." Immediately to the west of Ashcroft Acres, separated from it by only a dilapidated barbed wire fence, was the 100-acre farm of another celebrated son of Missouri, Byrd N.A. Busch, reputed to be the next heir to the Anheuser-Busch beer fortune. Busch was a lazy and largely useless individual whose only strategy in life seemed to be to gamble away his trust funds and wait for his wealthy relatives to die so he could inherit his fortune and move to the big city. Meanwhile, he was chronically short of cash and stuck on his farm, which was known locally as "Bud Liteacres."

The land along both sides of the border between Ashcroft Acres and Bud Liteacres formed a large, malodorous, unpleasant swamp. The swamp rendered about 10 percent of Ashcroft Acres, and fully 50 percent of Bud Liteacres, absolutely useless for any purpose to anyone but the local frogs. This had never been of concern to Ashcroft while he was involved in Missouri state politics, and Busch was likewise indifferent to the swamp, as he had no intention of engaging in farming or any other useful trade. However, when Ashcroft took his break from politics, Busch saw an opportunity to improve his land without having to do anything resembling physical labor himself and without having to spend any money.

One fine spring morning, Busch invited Ashcroft to join him for a cup of coffee at the local diner, the Reflux House of Grits. During the course of an extended conversation, Busch presented the following proposal:

> Busch: Tell you what I have in mind, Johnny boy. We need that swamp drained. You need it, and I need it even more.

> Ashcroft: I agree. And don't call me Johnny boy. I'm a lawyer. I'm a serious guy.

> Busch: Lighten up, Johnny boy. Switch to decaf. Anyway, here's my offer. You dig a drainage ditch along your side of the border between our farms stretching all the way to Stagnant Creek in the south. I figure that will be enough to drain both farms and make all the land useful. In return for that, plus $50,000, I will convey one-fourth of Bud Liteacres to you. You can have the 25 acres that abuts the current border between the two farms. We can go out and step it off now, if you like. You can pay me $5,000 as a down payment tomorrow. Ten

days after you complete the
ditch, I'll give you a deed to the
25 acres currently included in
Bud Liteacres and you can pay
me the remaining $45,000.

Ashcroft: Well I am surprised.
25 acres for $50,000 and a ditch.
That sounds like a pretty fair
deal for everyone. In fact, you
have a deal. Let's shake hands
on it and go mark off the portion
of Bud Liteacres I'm buying.

The two men shook hands on their agreement and proceeded directly to Bud Liteacres. Once there, they marked the 25 acres Busch intended to convey with a series of stakes, posts and marks carved on trees. The next day, Ashcroft paid Busch the $5,000 down payment upon which the two had agreed in their conversation.

Ashcroft then began to investigate ways to dig the drainage ditch required by his verbal agreement with Busch. He checked with a series of local excavation contractors, any one of whom was willing to do the job for $50,000. However, Ashcroft happened to own a bulldozer and a backhoe as part of the equipment on Ashcroft Acres. He also thought a stint of hard labor out of doors would help him forget the scandals surrounding the Clinton administration. So he spent the next 30 days manning the bulldozer and backhoe, cheerfully digging a ditch across the western edge of his own land to Stagnant Creek. In the process, he removed the barbed wire fence that marked the current border between Ashcroft Acres and Bud Liteacres. Since he contributed his own labor, his only out of pocket costs consisted of $5,000 for gasoline and vehicle maintenance. When Ashcroft completed the ditch, it did exactly what Busch predicted it would. It drained all the swampy land on both farms, effectively reclaiming what had been useless acreage.

Upon completion of the ditch, Ashcroft notified Busch by e-mail that he would be prepared to pay the remaining $45,000 in ten days as they had verbally agreed, and that he expected a deed to the 25 acre designated portion of Bud Liteacres at that time. He received a return voice mail message from Busch saying only, "See you in ten days, Johnny boy."

Ten days later, Ashcroft arrived at Busch's door with a cashier's check for $45,000, payable to Busch. Busch was nowhere to be found. The only person on the premises was Busch's caretaker, a large, unpleasant fellow named Bubba who had an annoying habit of carrying a shotgun everywhere he went. Bubba refused to accept the check. Instead, he handed Ashcroft the following handwritten note from Busch:

Dear Johnny boy,

I've been watching you digging
Like some hired hand.
You grunted and sweated
And drained both our lands.

But I've changed my mind
Though it seems such a pity
I'll give you no deed
I'm off to the city.

Please put back the fence.
You shouldn't have moved it.
And don't talk of contract.
You really can't prove it.

Sincerely yours,

/s/ Byrd

Byrd N. A. Busch

Ashcroft's initial reaction was the appearance on his face, for the first time, of the famous grimace with which we are all now so familiar. To this day, you can see it every time he appears on television. His second reaction was to consult his lawyer. You are that lawyer. Advise him.

QUESTION

1.   Ashcroft wants to know what rights and remedies, if any, he has against Busch. Remember that Ashcroft is not only a lawyer but a meticulous one. Accordingly, explain all his options and discuss any obstacles and the likelihood of success. Explain the reasons for your answer. (Approximately 70 minutes.)

THE BUSCH FAMILY SAGA CONTINUES

About two years later, Byrd N.A. Busch did indeed inherit the Anheuser-Busch family fortune. He reacted by behaving exactly as you would expect from such a scoundrel. He filled his life with high-stakes poker games, big cigars, expensive cars, high-fat food, and, of course, copious quantities of the golden beverage for which his family is so justly famous. Over the next 5 years, he proceeded to ruin his health with a combination of bad diet, smoking, lack of sleep, excessive alcohol consumption, and other vices not suitable for discussion in polite company.

In the last years of his life, Busch was nearly an invalid, which led some of his relatives to conclude that there is, indeed, some form of cosmic justice. He suffered from liver, kidney and heart ailments, as well as a painful case of gout. He sought help from relatives, but most of them despised him so thoroughly that they would not come to his aid. The lone exception was his favorite niece, Rose Busch. Rose was an auto mechanic by trade, but she was currently out of work. One day, as Rose was visiting her uncle, he explained the difficulties he was experiencing living on his own and predicted that he would not live much longer. He asked if she would consider moving into his mansion, cooking his meals, chauffeuring him around town, and attending to his medical needs, all for an indefinite period of time. "If you take care of old Uncle Byrd," the elder Busch said, "I'll see to it you don't regret it."

Two days later, Rose moved into a comfortable wing of the Busch family mansion. For the next six months, she provided food and transportation for her failing uncle and saw to it that he received adequate medical care. Her room and board was provided at her uncle's expense. At the end of six months, she found an envelope addressed to her on the kitchen table. It contained a promissory note signed by her uncle Byrd. The note included Byrd's written promise to pay Rose the sum of $5,000 and recited that the promise was "in consideration of much-appreciated service to me in this difficult time." Byrd was not present at the time, and the two never discussed the promissory note. A month later, Byrd N.A. Busch died without having paid the note.

ANOTHER QUESTION

2.   Assume Rose sues the estate of Byrd N.A. Busch for $5,000. What, if anything, will she recover? On what legal theory? Explain the reasons for your answer. (Approximately 25-30 minutes.)

DIFFERENT FACTS: CLINTON IS MORE FUN

But enough about Republicans. As you know, former President Bill Clinton took up residence in Westchester County, New York, and leased space for his office in New York City (more specifically, in Harlem). In case you have never been to the Big Apple, that's quite a lengthy commute. After eight years in the White House, Clinton firmly believed it was beneath his dignity to take public transportation or drive himself. He was convinced he needed, not just a ride, but a luxury-class, chauffeur-driven ride. He already had an assigned Secret Service agent willing to do the driving, but he needed a car. Given his congenital arrogance, he concluded only a Rolls Royce (or, as it is known to its devotees, a "Rolls") would do. So he placed the following ad in the *New York Times* and *Washington Post*, in capital letters so it would capture attention:

EX-PRESIDENT DESPERATELY NEEDS ROLLS
SUPPLY MY ROLLS AND GET THANKS OF GRATEFUL
NATION
ALSO WILLING TO CONSIDER COST PLUS 10% OR BEST
OFFER
WIRE, EMAIL OR PHONE PROPOSAL TO:

BILL CLINTON
OFFICES IN THE HOOD
NEW YORK, NEW YORK
1-800-LECHEROUS
bclinton@licentious.com

One of the people who noticed the ad was Pierre LeDough, who had operated a pastry shop (LeDough's of Capitol Hill) in Washington, D.C., during the Clinton administration. While he was President, Clinton, in fact, had been one of LeDough's best customers. Clinton, whose appetites are well known, had become absolutely addicted to LeDough's famous cinnamon rolls. He had ordered them at least once a week for White House breakfast meetings or photo opportunities, normally in quantities of 100, for delivery the day following the order. Since Clinton's departure from office, LeDough's pastry business had declined, and he had opened a used car lot as a sideline. The car business, Snootycars of

Georgetown, specialized in used but expensive luxury import automobiles. LeDough had sent Clinton a printed announcement when the dealership opened.

LeDough, however, assumed that Clinton's ad was about food, not cars. He figured Clinton's craving for cinnamon rolls had just kicked in, and he also thought he could revive his pastry business by becoming known as Clinton's cinnamon roll supplier. On top of everything else, 10% was his usual profit margin on cinnamon rolls—i.e., he sold them for $220 per hundred, and they cost him $200 per hundred to make. So he sent Clinton the following e-mail, neglecting, as most e-mailers do, to use any capitalization or punctuation whatsoever:

hi mr president

would love to supply your rolls—
willing to bid cost plus 10% with
other terms standard—if
acceptable phone 1800mobutta
and leave message or email
specifying delivery anytime with
minimum one-day notice

yours

pierre ledough proprietor
ledoughs of capitol hill and
snootycars of Georgetown

———

Clinton received the e-mail on December 1, 2001. On December 3, he replied to LeDough with the following e-mail, which, like LeDough's, followed the custom of omitting punctuation and capitalization:

hey pierre whassup man—cost
plus ten for the rolls suits me

fine—deliver to my office in
harlem december 5 10:00 am—
looking forward to it

yours

bill clinton

———————

I assume you can guess what happened on December 5 at 10:00 A.M. LeDough arrived at Clinton's office with 100 hot, fresh cinnamon rolls and a bill for $220. Clinton arrived with a suitcase full of leftover "soft money" from his presidential campaigns, expecting a Rolls Royce automobile to be parked out front. The two engaged in a heated discussion, in which LeDough insisted that they had a contract for cinnamon rolls and Clinton insisted they had a contract for a luxury car. Clinton would not accept the cinnamon rolls. LeDough would not deliver a car. The two reached impasse fairly quickly, and Clinton kept his money while LeDough kept his cinnamon rolls. As he walked away, LeDough muttered, "As a lying, double dealing, double crossing swindler, this Clinton guy is absolutely peerless."

Clinton and LeDough consulted their respective lawyers, and each eventually filed a claim against the other for breach of contract. LeDough, in the meantime, took his cinnamon rolls back to his shop and placed them in inventory with hundreds of others. He sold a lot of cinnamon rolls that day (all at $2.20 each), although it was impossible to determine precisely to whom he sold the rolls he had tendered to Clinton. At the end of the day, he had no cinnamon rolls left.

Clinton decided to do without a car. Between December 1, 2001 and December 15, 2001, only 10 used Rolls Royce automobiles were sold in the entire area between Washington D.C. and New York City. The wholesale cost of the cars ranged from $40,000 to $60,000, and the dealers in question invariably sold the cars at cost plus 20%.

MORE QUESTIONS

3.   Did Clinton and LeDough have a contract?[1] If so, was it for the sale of a car or for the sale of cinnamon rolls? Explain the reasons for your answer. (Approximately 40 minutes.)

4.   Assume Clinton and LeDough had a contract for cinnamon rolls. What damages, if any, may LeDough recover from Clinton? Explain the reasons for your answer. (Approximately 15 minutes.)

5.   Assume Clinton and LeDough had a contract for a car. What damages, if any, may Clinton recover from LeDough? Explain the reasons for your answer. (Approximately 15 minutes.)

---

[1]   In answering this question, assume that there is no problem with the statute of frauds, i.e., that the e-mails of the parties would qualify as any necessary writings.

CONTRACTS ESSAY EXAM #2

FACTS: THE HEIR TO THE THRONE

Imagine, if you will, that it is now 1999 and you do not know how the 2000 Presidential Election will turn out. George W. Bush ("George W"), is still just the son of the former President and now a candidate for the Presidency in his own right. George W has been seeking the Republican nomination for President for months, and he has distinguished himself primarily as a campaign fundraiser. His only drawback, of course, is that he is utterly without knowledge of, or experience in, national or international politics. The latter fact was made painfully obvious in a recent press conference, in which George W was unable, in response to reporters' questions, to name the leader of any foreign nation, any of the Justices of the Supreme Court of the United States, or any of the planets in our solar system. George W's advisers suggested to him that his education might be somewhat deficient and further suggested he take a crash course in national and international affairs.

George W went to his father, former President Bush, for advice, and the elder Bush suggested that George W enlist the aid of Henry Kissinger, the somewhat aged but well-respected former Secretary of State from the Nixon administration. George W telephoned Kissinger on October 1, 1999, and the conversation proceeded as follows:

Kissinger: Henry Kissinger, adviser to persons of greatness, at your service.

George W: Hank, you old sea dog. This is George W. Can I call you Hank? How are you?

Kissinger: I hate it when people call me Hank.

George W: Right you are, Hank. Listen, Hank. I have a problem. Some people seem to think I'm an intellectual lightweight and an ignoramus on policy matters.

Kissinger: Let's just say that Dan Quayle has never looked wiser or more erudite.

George W: Ha ha. That's a good one Hank. Listen, here's the deal. I need a tutor. All these foreign countries and foreign leaders have such funny names. It's now October 1, and, if I'm going to win the nomination and the Presidency and take office in January of 2001, I'm going to need constant tutoring from now through December 2000. That's a full fifteen months. If you will give me one two-hour tutorial per week over the next 15 months, I'll pay you $5,000 a month. I'll even come to you, so you don't have to travel or incur any expenses. I've got more corporate jets at my disposal than the Air Force has fighter planes, and I can go wherever I want whenever I want. We could have the sessions early on Monday mornings—say at 11:00 A.M.

Kissinger: What if you don't win the nomination? What if you drop out of the race early? Will I be left without a job?

George W: No way, Hank. You don't understand. I'm offering you a guaranteed job as my tutor in national and international affairs for an absolute minimum of fifteen months. No more, no less. You'll get a paycheck at the end of each month. And it only requires two hours a week. You can do anything else you want for the rest of each week. But I want you to commit now for the full fifteen months so I don't have to worry about this any more. So what do you say? You can start this week.

Kissinger paused for a moment and put down the phone. Even though he had managed to tolerate Richard Nixon, he did not like overgrown fraternity boys like George W very much. On the other hand, he had some experience tutoring famous politicians and knew the market for such educational services. Weekly tutoring sessions for even the most famous politicians did not normally bring anything close to $5,000 a month. The going market rate for comparable work was about $2,000 a month. In addition, it was clear that, given George W's willingness to come to Kissinger for the sessions, the deal required no out of pocket expenditures by Kissinger. Finally, Kissinger knew that his own services were not in as much demand as they had been in his heyday in the 1960's and 1970's, and he had absolutely nothing planned for the next fifteen months. Effectively, he was already retired. He decided he had nothing to lose by taking the deal. So he picked up the phone again and continued the conversation as follows:

> Kissinger: Okay, I am back.

> George W: Glad to hear it, Hank. I thought you went out for a beer.

> Kissinger: Unlikely. Anyway, I have thought it over and have decided to accept your offer. I am now your tutor, and I am at your disposal.

> George W: Wise move Hank. We're going to be a great team. See you Monday.

> Kissinger: I can hardly wait. Good-bye.

Kissinger hung up the phone, and he and George W had no further communications concerning the tutoring until the first Monday in October arrived. True to his word, George W arrived at Kissinger's door at the appointed time on the appointed day. Kissinger delivered a brilliant two-hour lecture on national and international politics, with which George W was extremely pleased. Thereafter, throughout October, November and December of 1999, the process was repeated each Monday. George W arrived at Kissinger's door at 11:00 A.M. and received a two-hour tutorial in the designated subjects.

The only problem was that George W had not yet paid Kissinger at the end of each month as promised. Indeed, he had not paid Kissinger at all. Kissinger became concerned and, on Tuesday of the last week of December, he sent George W a bill for $15,000 for three months of tutoring. Bush responded with the following telegram:

Dear Hank:

You're old and you're boring,
If I may be blunt,
And when dealing with me,
You should get your money up
front.

I'll pay you no money,
Neither salary nor tips.
As my father would say,
"Get lost! Read my lips."

--George W

P.S.   I won't be back.

QUESTIONS

You are Kissinger's attorney. He has come to you hopping mad. And watching Kissinger hop is not a pretty sight. He wants to know if he has a case against George W. Specifically, he wants your answers to the following questions:

1.   Is his agreement with George W enforceable? (Approximately 25 minutes)

2.   Assuming the answer to question 1. is "yes," what are his rights and remedies against George W? (Approximately 20-25 minutes)

3.   Assuming the answer to question 1. is "no," does he have any rights or remedies against George W? (Approximately 40 minutes)

Advise Kissinger. He's a demanding client, so state the reasons for your answers.

MORE FACTS: YO! WHAT ARE YOU LOOKIN' AT? THE CARPETBAGGER AND THE DONALD GO TO NEW YORK

For our next episode, we move to the great State of New York, where it is still 1999, and the results of the 2000 elections are unknown. Hillary Clinton is committed to a bid for the Democratic nomination to the U.S. Senate (though you do not yet know she will win both the nomination and the seat.) Donald Trump has announced his intention to seek the nomination of the Reform Party for President of the United States. (Okay. So you can predict how that one will come out.) Isn't that great? Hillary and the Donald in the same place at the same time.

Anyway, Hillary Clinton had just moved into her new home in Westchester County, New York, when her political advisers presented her with a problem. Their polls revealed that some of Hillary's earlier comments as First Lady—and particularly her statement that she "was not some woman sitting around baking cookies"—had offended working class New York voters. (Working class New Yorkers apparently remember their mommies' cookies very fondly.) Hillary decided that some form of political damage control was necessary, and the solution came to her when she noticed that the kitchen of her new million-dollar home was equipped with commercial ovens. She decided that opening a bakery would help soften her image. So she started a baking business under the name, "Hillary's Old Time Arkansas Irresistible Recipes," or "HOTAIR" for short. HOTAIR'S sales of cookies, pies and cakes were brisk from the outset, and word of Hillary's venture spread throughout New York.

One of the people who heard of Hillary's business was developer Donald Trump ("the Donald"), who was in the process of planning fundraising dinners to finance his campaign for the Reform Party nomination for the

Presidency. Specifically, the Donald already had two fundraising dinners scheduled at the Waldorf-Astoria in December of 1999, and he decided it would be delicious irony to have a Democrat like Hillary supply the desserts for both. The first was an ordinary $1000 a plate fundraising dinner with the theme "Dilettantes in Politics" ("the DIP dinner") scheduled for December 15. It was open to anyone who had the price of admission. The second was a dinner targeted to reach a special audience, the numerous members of weight loss organizations residing in the trendier sections of New York City. Its theme was "Belligerent Large and Oversized Advocates for Trump," and it was scheduled for December 23 ("the BLOAT dinner"). The Donald's idea was to let anyone in who could show a membership card from Weight Watchers or Jenny Craig, and then solicit contributions when they had eaten and were in a good mood.

The Donald reviewed the HOTAIR dessert catalogue and noticed that Hillary offered a variety of cookies. Traditional sugar cookies were available for those without dietary restrictions or concern for calories. For the weight-conscious or health-conscious, sugar-free gingerbread cookies were available. The catalogue stated that each type was available "in a variety of holiday and festive shapes." The Donald decided to inquire further and telephoned Hillary on Thanksgiving Day. The conversation went as follows:

> The Donald: Hello, gorgeous. This is the Donald calling. Say, can you make cookies shaped like me?

> Hillary: No. I don't have an oven big enough for your ego.

> The Donald: How about in the shape of a supermodel?

Hillary: Look, if you want a locker room conversation, I'll get Bill. Don't waste my time.

The Donald: Okay, okay. I need cookies for some political fundraisers. What do you recommend?

Hillary: I can make them in the shape of balloons. That usually offends people less than cookies shaped like dollar signs.

The Donald: Sounds good. Although one of the dinners is near Christmas. Can you make reindeer cookies?

Hillary: Sure. I'm married to an animal.

The Donald: That's fabulous, absolutely fabulous. But I'll need big quantities. I do everything big.

Hillary: I'm so impressed. Look, just write up an order when you've decided what you need. Then I'll tell you if I can help you.

The Donald: You will hear from me. Good bye.

On December 1, 1999, the Donald wrote Hillary the following letter:

TRUMP FOR PRESIDENT

"Because A Billion Isn't Enough"

PENTHOUSE—WHERE ELSE?

TRUMP TOWER

NEW YORK, NEW YORK (You need a Zip Code, I Don't Bother With You)

December 1, 1999

Ms. Hillary Clinton
HOTAIR
101 Carpetbagger Lane
Westchester County, New York

Dear Hillary:

Nice to talk to you yesterday. Please accept my orders for the following:

1. 300 Dozen HOTAIR Balloon traditional sugar cookies, @ $10.00 per dozen. Delivery by your truck on 12/15/99 to the DIP Dinner, Waldorf-Astoria, New York, New York, by 7:00 P.M. Payment terms: Cash on delivery.

2. 300 Dozen HOTAIR sugar-free gingerbread Reindeer cookies, @ $20.00 per dozen. Delivery by your truck on 12/23/99 to the BLOAT Dinner, Waldorf-Astoria, New York,

New York, by 7:00 P.M. Payment
terms: Cash on delivery.

If the foregoing terms are acceptable to you,
please sign the enclosed copy of this letter
and return it to me. Looking forward to doing
business wit' youse, I am

Sincerely
yours,

/s/ Donald
Trump

Donald Trump

Hillary received the letter on December 3 and promptly signed and returned a copy to the Donald. December is a busy season for bakers, but Hillary believed that the quantities and varieties the Donald had ordered were within her capacity to deliver under normal circumstances.

Alas, the circumstances proved to be anything but normal. The trouble began with the cookies for the DIP dinner scheduled for December 15. The preparation of HOTAIR sugar cookies required enormous amounts of sugar, and Hillary's storage capacity was limited. It was therefore her practice to order sugar on a weekly basis, and each week's shipment satisfied her baking needs for that week only. The problem was that, on December 5, 1999, the sugar producing nations of the world, in hitherto unheard of unity, announced their support for the Cuban regime of Fidel Castro, whose economy was utterly dependent upon sugar. As a gesture of support for Castro, the entire sugar cartel announced a sellers' boycott of the United States. Foreign sugar was unavailable in the U.S. at any price. While domestically produced sugar was, as always, readily available, its price skyrocketed immediately. By the next day, December 6, the price of sugar in the U.S. had increased by 2000 %. The result, for Hillary, was that the $10 per dozen price that had seemed so favorable for sugar cookies on December 1 was now so low that, if forced to perform the contract for the DIP dinner, HOTAIR would actually suffer a loss of $10 per dozen. While some businesses might have been able to weather such a loss, the Clintons' debts for legal fees for the Whitewater and impeachment investigations were so large that they were already on the very edge of insolvency. So Hillary telephoned the Donald:

Hillary: Hello, gorgeous, how are you? This is Hillary.

The Donald: Fabulous, absolutely fabulous. I just made yet another fortune in sugar futures. Have I got the golden touch or what?

Hillary: And so humble, too. Anyway, I have a problem. If I have to deliver sugar cookies to the DIP dinner at $10 per dozen, it will break me. I know you're not used to either honesty or mercy, but I need a price increase. How about $20 per dozen? That way, I break even, and that's all I'm asking.

The Donald: You're lucky I'm in a good mood. I made Merv Griffin beg. But

>   Christmas is coming. So okay.
>   We'll change the price to $20 a
>   dozen. Give my best to Bill.

> Hillary: Thanks. I'll send confirmation.

True to her word, Hillary sent a written confirmation of the price change to the Donald, and the Donald wrote "agreed," signed it, and sent it back to her. Hillary then acquired the sugar and other ingredients necessary to fill the Donald's order for sugar cookies for the DIP dinner. She baked the cookies on the evening of December 14 and the wee hours of the morning of December 15. She delivered the right quantity and the right kind of cookies to the Waldorf-Astoria by 7:00 P.M. on December 15. Once she had turned over the cookies, however, the Donald refused to pay more than the original contract price of $3000 (i.e., $10 per dozen). Hillary took the $3000 but promised the Donald that he would "hear from one of my ever-expanding battery of lawyers."

Hillary briefly had the impulse to refuse to perform her obligation to deliver cookies to the December 23 BLOAT Dinner, but her political advisers talked her out of the urge for vengeance. Since the cookies for that dinner were to be sugar-free, the worldwide sugar boycott of the U.S. presented no problem. However, she had a scheduling conflict. Months earlier, she had promised to deliver a speech on December 22 to one of her key support groups, Abrasive Washingtonians Fleeing Ugly Liaisons (or "AWFUL" for short). She decided she simply could not back out of the AWFUL speech. So she gathered all the ingredients, made the dough, stamped out the raw cookies, and left them on trays by the oven on the evening of December 22. As she had no one else to turn to, she instructed her husband, Bill Clinton, to put the cookies in the oven at 1:00 A.M. on December 23 and remove them at 2:00 A.M. Bill agreed to do exactly that. He always does what he's supposed to do, right?

When the appointed time came, Bill put the cookies in the oven. Unfortunately, he then became distracted watching reruns of Barbara Walters' television interview with Monica Lewinsky. (You expected sugar-free cookies to hold Bill's interest?) By the time Bill came to his senses, the cookies had been in the oven for four hours and were hopelessly burned. To make matters worse, there were no ingredients for a new batch of cookies. Upon her return in the late morning of December 23, Hillary realized the situation was hopeless. She telephoned the Donald and told him unequivocally that she would be unable to deliver any cookies to the BLOAT dinner that evening.

The Donald was angry but undaunted. He searched for an alternative cookie supplier in New York City and the surrounding suburbs of New York, New Jersey and Connecticut. But two days before Christmas, all the usual suppliers were fully committed to other customers. By sheer luck, however, Donald encountered Charlton Heston, the actor and President of the National Rifle Association, on the afternoon of December 23. As it happened, Heston had 300 dozen reindeer cookies left over from an extremely unsuccessful National Rifle Association Christmas dinner the previous evening. (Apparently the theme, "Peace on Earth, Good Will to Man" was not a hit with N.R.A. members.) Donald paid Heston $30 a dozen for the N.R.A. reindeer cookies, which represented a substantial premium over the price Donald would have had to pay for an order placed with a commercial supplier in advance of the holidays. But Heston delivered on time, and the Donald had his cookies for the BLOAT dinner. The only real problem at the dinner arose from the fact that the N.R.A. cookies differed in one key respect from Hillary's cookies. Each of the N.R.A. reindeer cookies had a small target (i.e., a bull's eye) etched in frosting on the side of the reindeer. While this presented no problem for most of the guests, ten of them were animal activists with tender sensibilities. The sight of the N.R.A. cookies filled them with righteous indignation, which led them to break all the windows in the Waldorf-Astoria ballroom. The Donald's campaign was forced to settle the hotel's damage claim for $50,000.

MORE QUESTIONS

4.   Under Article 2 of the Uniform Commercial Code, what rights and remedies, if any, does Hillary have against the Donald arising out of their agreement relating to the DIP Dinner? Would your answer have been different under the common law of contracts? Explain the reasons for your answers. (Approximately 40 minutes)

5.   Under Article 2 of the Uniform Commercial Code, what rights and remedies, if any, does the Donald have against Hillary arising out of their agreement relating to the BLOAT Dinner? Would your answer have been different under the common law of contracts? Explain the reasons for your answers. (Approximately 40 minutes)

CONTRACTS ESSAY EXAM #3

"FACTS"

Imagine, if you will, that by February of 1998, Janet Reno had grown weary of her job as Attorney General of the United States. Faced with yet another subpoena from a Congressional committee investigating the Whitewater scandal and further demands for a special prosecutor to investigate the phone solicitations conducted by the Clinton campaign, Janet decided she had had enough of Bill and Hillary Clinton's problems. She resigned from her post, and decided to pursue a career as an entrepreneur in the private sector. To that end, she leased a two-story commercial building in Encino, California. On the ground floor, she planned to open a celebrity theme restaurant called "Planet Janet." Her hope was to follow the lead of the pioneering theme restaurants (e.g., Planet Hollywood, the Hard Rock Café, etc.) and serve low-grade junk food at dramatically inflated prices.

Her ambitions for the second floor were even less noble. She planned to open a gambling den to be known as "Reno's Casino of Encino." (Gambling had just been legalized in California, and, thanks to some of her more unsavory professional acquaintances, Janet had acquired sufficient expertise to operate a gaming establishment.)

Janet's hope was to open both the casino and the restaurant with a huge Independence Day party on July 4, 1998. Accordingly, her days were filled with the usual series of transactions necessary to prepare and open new businesses. Several transactions were of particular interest.

First, Janet decided she needed a truly distinctive piece of art to adorn the entrance of Planet Janet. She had previously received a two-ton block of granite as a gift from a New York mobster, who had hoped she would use it as a headstone in the event of an untimely demise. Janet now decided, however, to use the stone to create a larger-than-life statue of herself to be placed near the door of the restaurant. The only problem was that Janet had no artistic talent whatsoever. Accordingly, she began searching for the services of a sculptor.

Eventually, Janet located a thoroughly mediocre sculptor, Hart O. Stone, who was among a rather large group of similar "artists" currently eking out a living carving small replicas of Mt. Rushmore and selling them to tourists in Western South Dakota. On March 1, Janet and Hart agreed by telephone that Hart would relocate to Encino and carve "a two-ton granite Janet" out of Janet's granite block. Hart was to complete the project in three months (i.e., by June 1). He was to be paid a total of $10,000 for his services[2], which was in line with the market rate for sculptors of Hart's rather minimal skill level. Payment was to be made upon completion of the statue.

Hart promptly moved to Encino and began carving away on the block of granite. By mid-April, Hart had completed half of the necessary work. Alas, however, artists are sensitive souls. The day after watching a documentary on the life of Picasso on public television, Hart realized that he was a third-rate hack and concluded that his life had become pointless. Accordingly, he refused to proceed further with the statue and retreated to a Hare Krishna monastery in Marin County. Fortunately for Janet, Hart's brother, Sandy Stone, lived on the coast near Malibu. Sandy spent most of his time surfing, but, much like his brother, he was a sculptor of somewhat modest talents. Sandy offered to complete the remaining half of the statue for a fee of $6,000.

---

[2]   Please do not analyze this transaction as a sale of goods under Article 2 of the U.C.C. Janet already owns the granite block. All Hart is supplying is services. Don't say I never gave you anything for free.

QUESTIONS

1.   If Janet declines Sandy's offer to complete the statue, can she successfully sue Hart for specific performance of the original agreement? Explain the reasons for your answer. (Approximately 25 minutes.)

2.   Suppose Janet accepts Sandy's offer to complete the statue, and that he does so. Suppose further that Janet pays Sandy in full but pays Hart nothing. Does Hart have any rights and remedies against Janet? Explain the reasons for your answer. (Approximately 35 minutes.)

MORE "FACTS"

Of course, Janet was even more concerned about the food to be served at Planet Janet than about its ambience. Her plan was to build her restaurant around a particularly tasty half-pound char-broiled cheeseburger called the "Flaming Wacoburger." She knew she would need a large quantity of ground beef for her gala opening on July 4, so she began searching for a supplier early in March. On March 20, she entered into a written forward contract with Hudson Foods, Inc. for 10,000 pounds of fresh ground beef to be delivered in the early morning hours on July 4, 1998, at a price of $1.00 per pound.

Secure in the belief that her restaurant needs would be satisfied, Janet turned her attention to Reno's Casino of Encino. Professional gamblers have, in recent years, developed a rather euphemistic vocabulary to describe their peculiar trade, which is now known as the "gaming industry." Every casino must have a manager of general operations, and such individuals were once known as "chief thugs", "legbreakers," "major gorillas," "lead sharks," or other names not fit to print. The job title is now "Manager Assigned to Grab the Gain Off The Tables," or "MAGGOTT" for short.   Janet needed a MAGGOTT in place for the opening of her casino, and she began to interview candidates for the job by telephone.

Janet's search focussed initially on former Clinton aide George Stephanopolous.   After several telephone conversations, Janet sent George the following letter:

JANET RENO
RENO'S CASINO OF ENCINO
ENCINO, CALIFORNIA
April 2, 1998

Mr. George Stephanopolous
Georgy Porgy Consulting Services
Beltway Bandit Building
Washington, D.C.

Dear George:

As I mentioned to you by phone, your work for President Clinton convinced me that you had developed the skills of a small time MAGGOTT. I believe you are now ready to be a MAGGOTT on a grand scale. Accordingly, I hereby offer you the position of MAGGOTT of Reno's Casino of Encino on the following terms. Your employment will commence on July 1, 1998, and your initial term of employment will expire six months later on January 1, 1999. Thereafter, the contract may be renewed on whatever terms are acceptable to both of us. Your salary for the six-month initial term will be $30,000. You will work the night shift (7:00 P.M. to 3:00 A.M.) six nights a week, excluding Sunday night. I will provide health insurance benefits comparable to those prevailing in the

Encino area. The nature of your duties is familiar to you from our previous conversations. If this offer is acceptable to you, please make a photocopy of this letter and sign it in the blank space below my signature. I will hold this offer open until April 30, 1998.

> Sincerely yours,
> /s/ Janet Reno
> Janet Reno, Proprietor
> Reno's Casino of Encino

Janet's letter struck young George as a gift from heaven. Since leaving the Clinton administration, he had been unable to find work, and his "consulting firm," Georgy Porgy Consulting Services, was little more than a shell. Upon receiving Janet's letter on April 5, he immediately made a photocopy, signed his name at the bottom, properly stamped and addressed it to Janet, and deposited it in the mail at the Washington D.C. post office at 11:46 P.M. on April 5. Janet did not receive the communication from George until April 10. Meanwhile, on April 6, it came to Janet's attention through a confidential informant that George had once made rather uncomplimentary remarks about Socks, the White House cat. In a fit of rage, Janet sent George the following letter:

JANET RENO
RENO'S CASINO OF ENCINO
ENCINO, CALIFORNIA
April 6, 1998

Mr. George Stephanopolous
Georgy Porgy Consulting Services
Beltway Bandit Building
Washington, D.C.

Dear George:

It has come to my attention that you do not have the morals to be even a low-level professional gambler, let alone a full-fledged MAGGOTT. Accordingly, I hereby revoke the offer made to you by letter dated April 2 of this year.

Sincerely yours,
/s/ Janet Reno
Janet Reno, Proprietor
Reno's Casino of Encino

Before receiving Janet's letter, George had already packed up and moved to Encino in anticipation of his new job. Janet's letter was forwarded to him from Washington, and he received it on April 20. He called Janet and insisted that they "had a deal" and that he was willing to perform, but Janet was adamant. She absolutely refused to employ him. On June 30, George accepted a job as a male stripper at Chippendale's of Encino. He worked the night shift, and was quite popular with the customers. He earned $20,000 between July 1, 1998 and January 1, 1999. Never mind the details.

It has no doubt occurred to you, Gentle Reader, that Janet is still in need of a MAGGOTT. Remain calm. Janet is in control, as always. On April 30, Janet sent a letter to Edwin Edwards, the former Governor of Louisiana, offering him the job of MAGGOTT at Reno's Casino of Encino for the period July 1, 1998-January 1, 1999 on precisely the same terms (including salary, hours, and insurance) that had been offered to George. Edwards received the letter on May 2 and dispatched an appropriate acceptance later the same afternoon, which Janet received with great pleasure on May 5. Edwards commenced work on July 1 as scheduled, and he was in attendance at the grand opening of Reno's Casino of Encino on July 4.

Unfortunately, the grand opening did not proceed as planned. The casino opened as scheduled, but the same was not true of the restaurant, Planet Janet. On the evening of July 3, Janet's supplier, Hudson Foods, Inc., discovered that the entire shipment of ground beef destined for Planet Janet was contaminated with *e.coli.* bacteria and utterly unfit for shipment, let alone human consumption. The entire beef inventory of Hudson was destroyed forthwith, and Hudson informed Janet on the morning of July 4 that it would be unable to deliver the ground beef. Janet searched desperately for an alternative supplier, but was unable to find one who could deliver on July 4. The best alternative she could find was a supplier known as Jagged Claw Meats, and she arranged to buy 10,000 pounds of ground beef from Jagged Claw at the prevailing market price of $2.00 per pound. Through extraordinary efforts, Jagged Claw managed to deliver the beef on July 5. Of course, this meant that Planet Janet opened a day late, and Janet believes that she lost $20,000 in opening night profits. (Average daily profits for the nearby Burger King are around $5,000; the local Hard Rock Cafe averages around $25,000 per day in profits.) To make matters worse, Bill Clinton had traveled all the way from Washington to attend the July 4 opening of Planet Janet, with dreams of Flaming Wacoburgers in his head. When the restaurant did not open, he was sorely disappointed. When he realized he had to fly back to Washington on the morning of July 5 without his quota of junk food, he became sorely ticked off. Using a little known law that permitted executive revocation of pension benefits for "demonstrated moral turpitude", Clinton ordered the forfeiture of Janet's accrued federal pension benefits, which were vested and worth $50,000 before Clinton's order.

To make matters even worse, Edwin Edwards became a source of difficulty in late September of 1998. Edwin had performed admirably as Janet's MAGGOTT for the months of July, August and September at the agreed salary. However, following his indictment in late September on unrelated matters, he suddenly felt a compelling urge for greater income. Accordingly, he informed Janet on September 28 that he would work no longer than September 30 unless his monthly salary was doubled, from $5000 per month to $10,000 per month. The reasons he assigned were: (A) That, without his silver-haired good looks and easy charm, the business was doomed; and (B) That the health insurance benefits she provided were inadequate because the insurer refused to pay for his lunches of crawfish etouffe. (With the easy guile of an experienced politician, Edwards asserted, with a straight face, that daily doses of crawfish etouffe are of medicinal value.) The doubling of his salary, Edwin argued, was an appropriate settlement of his claim for breach of Janet's promise to provide health insurance benefits. As no alternate qualified candidates for the position of MAGGOTT were available at the time, Janet agreed to Edwin's proposal. However, when payday came, she paid him only the original salary of $5000 per month.

QUESTIONS

3. What rights and remedies, if any, does George have against Janet? Explain the reasons for your answer. (Approximately 35 minutes.)

4. What rights and remedies, if any, does Janet have against Hudson Foods, Inc.? Explain the reasons for your answer. (Approximately 40 minutes.)

5. What rights and remedies, if any, does Edwin have against Janet?   Explain the reasons for your answer. (Approximately 25-30 minutes.)

CONTRACTS ESSAY EXAM #4

THE SLEAZE FACTOR UNCHAINED

Once the 1996 election was over, Bill and Hillary Clinton could abandon the thin veneer of devotion to the public good that they had assumed during the campaign. With their power secure, they felt free to return to the shameless advancement of their own interests and that of their close friends. Bill, of course, had enjoyed running for President much more than he enjoyed being President. Accordingly, he effectively delegated the task of running the country to Hillary, who was more qualified for the job anyway. This enabled Bill to pursue a variety of purely private projects.[3]

Much of Bill's time was devoted to a private, non-profit charitable foundation (of which he was chairman) set up to assist the numerous friends, aides and associates of the Clintons who had been indicted in recent years. The foundation was called "Felons Relying Exclusively on Elvis,"[4] or "F.R.E.E." for short. Bill was the principal fund-raiser for the foundation and, in that capacity, made numerous calls and visits to potential contributors. One of his most important phone calls was made to a wealthy industrialist, I.M. Fatcatt. Bill called Fatcatt on December 15 and launched into his standard pitch.

"Good morning, Sir," said Bill. "I'm Bill Clinton, as seen on T.V. Perhaps you saw my debate. This morning I am asking you to contribute to F.R.E.E., an organization devoted to helping poor unfortunate victims of

---

[3]   I.e., you are to assume that, in all of the negotiations and transactions that follow, Bill is acting as a private citizen, not as a representative of the government of the United States.

[4]   I remind the historically challenged that "Elvis" was the nickname given to Bill Clinton by the press corps in a previous election campaign.

prosecutorial overzealousness. Sir, many of these people are being persecuted—even threatened with jail—for no better reason than their friendship with me and slightly stunted moral sensibilities. But this is America, and no one should suffer discrimination simply because of some slight moral depravity like a tendency toward larceny...,"

At this point, Fatcatt interrupted Clinton. (Fatcatt did not get all that money by being a patient man.) "I know who you are and I know what you want," said Fatcatt. "I will give you $20,000, but it will have to be after January 1."

Bill was so accustomed to completing his standard speech he was unable to resist continuing with it, even after Fatcatt's interruption. "And as an incentive," continued Bill, "we can offer free gifts to our contributors. At the $10,000 level, you get a coffee mug with my picture on it. At the $20,000 level, you get a golf umbrella embossed with the presidential seal. At the $50,000 level, my barber will give you a haircut aboard Air Force One on the runway at Los Angeles International Airport."

Once again, Fatcatt interrupted. "Keep your silly trinkets," said Fatcatt. "I don't care about them. I already told you I'd give you $20,000. So take your doctor's advice and save your vocal cords. I will pay by the end of January."

"January 31st it is," replied Bill. "And thank you for making the world a little safer for minor felons from Arkansas. Have a nice day."

The same day (December 15), Bill sent Fatcatt a small post card with the title "Pledge Card", the text of which read as follows:

YES! I want to contribute to
F.R.E.E. and save the friends of
Bill and Hillary. I promise to
contribute _____, payable on
_____.

Sincerely,

_____
(Signature)

Fatcatt filled in the blanks on the card, designating $20,000 as the amount of his contribution and January 31, 1997 as the date it was due, signed the card, and returned it to Bill.

Bill turned out to be a successful fund-raiser, and, by December 30, he had collected pledge cards from numerous contributors reflecting total pledges in excess of one million dollars. Between January 1 and January 30, 1997, Bill, on behalf of F.R.E.E., entered into a series of contracts. First, he signed a written, one year lease of office space for F.R.E.E. in a Little Rock office tower, at a monthly rental of $10,000. Second, he hired a secretary (under an oral contract terminable at will) at a monthly salary of $1500. Third, he hired F. Lee Bailey to provide legal representation for the indicted "friends of Bill" who were F.R.E.E.'s intended beneficiaries. Bailey demanded (and Bill executed) a retainer agreement providing for a retainer of $50,000 in cash (payable on February 15), plus 12 cases of Scotch whiskey, each worth $200, and an hourly billing rate of $500. Fourth, Bill bought F.R.E.E. a "corporate membership" in Deliverance Dunes, an exclusive Little Rock golf club, signing an agreement committing F.R.E.E. to pay monthly dues of $2,000 for a minimum of one year.

On January 30, 1997, Fatcatt watched a television broadcast of one of Bill's news conferences. During the course of answering questions from the press, Bill once again used a phrase, "building a bridge to the Twenty-first Century", that he had coined and used repeatedly during the 1996 campaign. Fatcatt decided that anyone who repeated a metaphor that lame as frequently as Bill did deserved to have all his friends go to jail. Accordingly, on January 31st, Fatcatt telephoned Bill and repudiated his pledge of $20,000 to F.R.E.E.

QUESTION

1.   Assume that Bill, on behalf of F.R.E.E., sues Fatcatt for breach of the promise to pay $20,000. What, if anything, will Bill recover? State the reasons for your answer. (Approximately 45-50 minutes)

SLEAZE FACTOR II—THE NIGHTMARE CONTINUES

Even after Fatcatt's repudiation, Bill had more than enough pledges to proceed with his plans for F.R.E.E. He decided that the Little Rock office of F.R.E.E. needed an office manager. As nepotism had never troubled Bill, he contacted his brother, Roger Clinton, who was employed at the time as a singer in the cocktail lounge of the Dew Drop Inn on the outskirts of Little Rock. Bill and Roger met for lunch on February 1.

"Hey, Little Brother," Bill began. "Why don't you come to work for F.R.E.E. as our office manager? I'll pay you $2,000 a month plus medical insurance."

"How long would it last?" replied Roger. "Right now, I'm making $2,000 a month singing at the Dew Drop Inn. I can walk away anytime, but they've guaranteed me another two years if I want it. Can you match that?"

"Hey, who knows how long anything or anyone will last?" replied Bill. "Maybe ten years, maybe forever. Maybe you'll die tomorrow. Trust me. It's permanent. I'm your brother. I'll take care of you."

"I guess I can trust you," replied Roger. "After all, you are a famous politician. But I will need $3,000 a month, plus medical insurance. $2,000 is not enough."

"Okay. I appreciate your trust, and I feel your pain. $3,000 a month it is," responded Bill. "Welcome aboard. You are now a F.R.E.E. man."

Flushed with filial feeling, Roger immediately quit his job at the Dew Drop Inn, put his Hawaiian shirts and ukulele in storage, and took his business suits out of the winter closet in preparation for his new job working for his brother. Unfortunately, his confidence was misplaced. A few days after his lunch meeting with Roger, Bill decided to give the office manager job to one Jennifer Flowers, for reasons which need not concern us. He left a note for Roger which read:

> "Roses are red, just like scarlet
> tanagers. You have no job,
> 'cause I don't need two
> managers. Go back to the band,
> you lounge lizard.
>
> --Bill"

After receiving Bill's note, Roger tried to find work in the music business, as well as in a variety of offices, but neither the Dew Drop Inn nor anyone else would hire him for the next several years.

QUESTION

2.   Suppose Roger sues Bill, claiming breach of an employment contract with a minimum ten year

term.   Will his action succeed?   Can he recover anything on any legal theory?   State the reasons for your answer. (Approximately 55 minutes)

SLEAZE FACTOR III--THE FINAL FRONTIER

In addition to his work for F.R.E.E., Bill devoted substantial time to another venture, this time for profit. Bill knew one product better than any other. No, not cheeseburgers. We are talking about hair spray. Late at night in his basement, Bill had been manufacturing a particularly potent hair spray, which he began to market under the name, "Slick Willie's Whitewater Slick-Back."[5] Bill could make a bottle of Slick-Back for about a dollar and sell it for a standard price of $2.50. He actually sold quite a lot of it, and he shortly took steps to increase his production.

When he had been dealing in hair spray for about a year, Bill received a phone call from the owner of the largest hair salon in his home town, Lamar's of Little Rock.   Lamar was always looking for new hair care products to peddle to his genteel clients, and he asked Bill to send him a proposal for a deal on 1000 bottles of Slick-Back. Bill replied with the following letter:

FROM THE DESK OF WILLIAM JEFFERSON CLINTON
PURVEYOR OF FINE HAIR CARE PRODUCTS

March 1, 1997

Dear Lamar:

I am pleased to offer you 1000 bottles of Slick Willie's Whitewater Slick-Back at a special volume discount price of

---

[5]   The historically challenged are further reminded that "Slick Willie" is another press corps nickname for Bill Clinton.

$2.00 per bottle. That's fifty
cents off my standard price, so
act now. I will hold this offer
open until noon on March 15. I
can deliver within 5 days of
acceptance, with payment due on
delivery. You may respond by
mail or by phone. Hoping to hear
from you, I am

Sincerely yours,

/s/ William J.
Clinton

William Jefferson
Clinton

Lamar received the letter on March 3 and called Bill
on March 7. "About your letter...," Lamar began.

"Oh that," interrupted Bill. "I've changed my mind.
The deal is off. I revoke any and all proposals. There's no
reason for me to discount my price."

"You can't do that," retorted Lamar. "I am
accepting the offer as of now, and I am sending you a
letter confirming that." True to his word, Lamar sent Bill
a letter "accepting your offer of March 1," and Bill
received the letter on March 10. Bill, however, refused to
supply Lamar with any hair spray at any price. As it
happens, there was only one hair care product on the
market with holding power comparable to Slick-Back. It
was manufactured by Jimmy Johnson, coach of the
Miami Dolphins football team, and it was marketed under
the name, "Jimmy J's Miracle Miami Mousse." After
unsuccessfully exhorting Bill to supply him with Slick-
Back, Lamar ordered 1000 bottles of Jimmy's concoction

on March 20. Jimmy immediately accepted the order. The agreed price was Jimmy's standard price of $3.00 per bottle. (Jimmy never gives discounts. Jimmy also never gives an inch.)

On April 1, Bill received another order for Slick-Back, this time from a smaller haircutting business, Ferdinand's of Fayetteville. Ferdinand submitted a written order for 100 bottles of Slick-Back at Bill's standard price of $2.50 per bottle, payable on delivery. Bill accepted the order in writing and was in the process of packaging it for shipment when he received a further communication from Ferdinand. Ferdinand notified Bill that he had developed an allergy to hair and was forced to retire from his chosen profession. Accordingly, Ferdinand refused to accept or pay for any Slick-Back. Bill put the bottles he had set aside for Ferdinand back in his inventory, intending to sell them to other customers. Because all bottles of Slick-Back look alike, Bill cannot determine today whether the specific bottles once set aside for Ferdinand have been sold in subsequent transactions or remain in his inventory.

QUESTIONS

3. (a) Do Lamar and Bill have a contract?

    (b) Assuming Lamar and Bill do have a contract, what, if anything,
        may Lamar recover for its breach?

    State the reasons for your answers. (Approximately 35 minutes)

4. Does Bill have any legal remedy against Ferdinand? If so, what relief will he obtain? Explain the reasons for your answers. (Approximately 30 minutes)

CONTRACTS ESSAY EXAM #5

FACTS

Old McDonald had a farm. And on this farm McDonald grew crops and raised the usual variety of merry critters. But McDonald was sick of work that made his back sore and decided to become a land speculator like everyone else. Fortunately for McDonald, his land was located just outside the city limits of New Babylon, the largest city in the State of Disarray. Because of New Babylon's rapid growth in recent years, the McDonald farm was a prime prospect for real estate development. A simple ad McDonald placed in a local paper generated literally dozens of inquiries from parties interested in buying the farm. After negotiating by telephone with a number of developers of apartments, condominiums, single family homes, and shopping centers, McDonald came to the realization that, if you put twenty real estate developers in a room, they would be unlikely to have twenty dollars cash between them. So McDonald decided to enter more serious negotiations with the city of New Babylon, which had plenty of cash as a result of its 10% sales tax on nearly everything. McDonald guessed that his land was worth at least $400,000, so he decided he might as well ask the city (whose officials were known for their gullibility) for $500,000. On June 1, he hand-delivered a letter to the city of New Babylon in which he offered to sell his farm for $500,000 cash. The letter contained a proper legal description of the farm, and it specified a closing date of July 1 for payment of the price and delivery of a deed. It also contained the following paragraph: "This here is a real good deal, so I ain't lowering my price and I ain't holding the offer open long. In fact, you must accept by June 10 or this offer expires."

On June 3, the city council of New Babylon met in emergency session and approved the purchase of the McDonald farm on the terms stated in McDonald's letter.

As authorized by the Council, the Mayor of New Babylon, Karl Klutz, prepared a letter accepting McDonald's offer. Given Klutz' usual ruthless bureaucratic efficiency, it took several days to get the letter in final form. However, on June 8, Klutz deposited the letter at the New Babylon Post Office, paid the postal clerk the proper postage, and instructed the clerk to send the letter by certified mail, return receipt requested. The letter arrived at McDonald's farm on June 10, and the letter carrier obtained a written receipt for it from McDonald. This receipt was then returned to Klutz.

Before the letter arrived, however, McDonald had been a busy little bumpkin. Back on June 7, he had been contacted by Danny DiOxin, the President of the Glowing Ooze Toxic Waste Disposal Company. DiOxin, a rather flamboyant character, was interested in buying the McDonald farm for use as a waste disposal site, and, in casual conversations with McDonald, he kept saying things like, "Yep. This looks like a great place to dump a lot of sludge." and "Looks like this place is worth somewhere in seven figures." With visions of (slightly radioactive) dollars dancing in his brain, McDonald concluded his prospects for a deal were better with DiOxin than with the city of New Babylon. Though McDonald and DiOxin had not yet reached a final agreement, on June 9, McDonald sent a telegram to the city, which read as follows: "Offer to sell land is hereby revoked. Have found better deal. I'm going to be the trash king." This telegram arrived at Mayor Klutz' office on the afternoon of June 9. When the city's acceptance letter arrived at McDonald farm the next day, he threw it in a drawer, called Klutz and told the Mayor, "Stop kidding yourself. You have no deal."

QUESTION

1.   On June 15, the city of New Babylon filed an action against McDonald in the local state court. The city sought an order of specific performance directing

McDonald to convey his farm to the city and enjoining McDonald from conveying it to anyone else.[6] Should the city's action succeed? State the reasons for your answer. (Approximately 15 minutes)

MORE FACTS

Assume that the city of New Babylon won its suit against McDonald and that McDonald, in compliance with the order of the court, conveyed the farm to the city. Why would the city want a farm? The answer is obvious—as a site for a casino. The city of New Babylon had been licensed by the State of Disarray to develop, build and operate the world's largest land-based casino. Of course, the city had no idea how to do any of that. For that reason, the city entered into a partnership with Pariah's, Inc., a well-known developer, builder, and operator of casinos. Under the partnership agreement between Pariah's and the city, Pariah's was obligated to act as the prime contractor for the construction of the casino and to operate the casino once it was completed. In return, Pariah's was to receive 50% of the casino's net profits. (The city, quite obviously, was entitled to the remaining 50%.)

By July 1, Pariah's was busy lining up suppliers and subcontractors for the construction of the casino building. The project required a certain amount of excavation and foundation work, and Pariah's awarded the excavation subcontract to Sinkhole, Inc. In a written subcontract, Sinkhole agreed to perform all necessary excavation and grading work for $100,000, a figure which, in fact, represented the reasonable value of the work in question. Payment was due upon completion of the work, which was scheduled for September 1. Sinkhole began performing the subcontract on July 15.

---

[6] In its pleadings, the city recited its ability and willingness to tender the $500,000 purchase price immediately.

While Sinkhole was busy digging away, Pariah's began contracting for the materials and services that would be required once the excavation work was complete. The plans for the casino called for a heavy structural steel frame, and Pariah's therefore needed a structural steel subcontractor. On July 16, Pariah's entered into a written contract with Hot Rivet Constructors under which that company agreed to supply all labor and materials necessary for the construction of the steel frame for the building. The contract price was $500,000, and the deadline for completion of the frame was September 30. Payment was due 30 days from completion of the work.

While Pariah's planned to have its own employees actually lay the bricks for the building, it nevertheless needed a brick supplier. On July 17, Pariah's entered into a written contract with the Thick Brick Company for the purchase and sale of 400,000 bricks. The contract price was $1.00 per brick, and the contract required delivery of the entire order on October 30. Payment was due upon delivery.

The month of August was not a good one for anybody. On August 1, a fire swept through the storage facility where Sinkhole kept all its earthmoving equipment. Sinkhole's equipment was completely destroyed. To make matters worse, the equipment was uninsured, and Sinkhole did not have sufficient capital to afford replacement equipment. While Sinkhole had already completed precisely half of the excavation work required by its subcontract with Pariah's, the loss of its equipment completely disabled Sinkhole from further performance under the subcontract. On August 5, Sinkhole delivered a letter to Pariah's containing Sinkhole's profound apology and formal notification that it was unable to perform the remaining half of the subcontract. Pariah's responded by refusing to pay Sinkhole anything. On August 6, heavy rains caused a large pile of dirt that Sinkhole had left at the construction site to collapse on a trailer owned by Pariah's and used as an on-site office. Pariah's was forced to replace the trailer, at a cost of $5,000.

Sinkhole's default left Pariah's in something of a bind. Pariah's knew that, if it could not complete the excavation work by the scheduled completion date of September 1, the delayed opening of the casino would cost it hundreds of thousands of dollars. However, at such short notice, there was only one available substitute excavation subcontractor, Gouge'em, Inc., an outfit known to be slightly on the expensive side. Because Gouge'em claimed it would be required to work its crews overtime in order to complete the remaining half of the excavation work by September 1, its price for doing so was $75,000. Pariah's concluded it had no reasonable alternative but to contract with Gouge'em at that price, and it did so on August 10. Gouge'em completed the second half of the excavation work on time, and Pariah's paid Gouge'em in a timely fashion.

On August 11, Pariah's received a second unpleasant surprise. Specifically, Pariah's received a telephone call from the Thick Brick Company. The president of Thick Brick quite apologetically informed the president of Pariah's that a world-wide shortage of the clay used to make bricks had caused a sharp rise in Thick Brick's own production costs. As a result, strict performance of Thick Brick's contract with Pariah's would literally drive Thick Brick out of business. Accordingly, the president of Thick Brick asked the president of Pariah's to approve an increase in the contract price from $1.00 to $1.25 per brick. At that rate, the president of Thick Brick thought he could break even, although Thick Brick would still not make a profit on the subcontract. Reluctantly, the president of Pariah's agreed to the price change, and the parties executed an appropriate memorandum reflecting the modification on August 15.

If August was bad, September was even worse. On September 15, the president of Pariah's received another call from the president of Thick Brick. This time, the latter was combative, not apologetic. The president of Thick Brick told the president of Pariah's that Thick Brick was now selling bricks for as high as $2.00 apiece, and that Thick Brick now unequivocally refused to perform the supply contract with Pariah's at either the original or modified price. The president of Pariah's then consulted several of his friends with expertise in the brick manufacturing industry, all of whom told him that the current market price of bricks was ranging from $1.50 to $2.00 apiece, and that the current market conditions were likely to last for two to three years. After several unsuccessful attempts to persuade Thick Brick to perform, Pariah's arranged a substitute contract with another manufacturer, Quick Brick, Inc. On September 30, Pariah's and Quick Brick executed a written contract requiring Quick Brick to deliver 400,000 bricks on October 30 at a price of $1.50 per brick, payable on delivery. (As things turned out, the brick manufacturing experts were mistaken in their predictions. In early October, vast quantities of clay suitable for bricks were discovered in rural Georgia, and, by October 30, the availability of cheap raw materials had driven the price of bricks back down to $1.00 apiece.)

By the end of September, Pariah's was experiencing severe cash flow shortages of its own and was becoming increasingly concerned over the cost of the casino project. Hot Rivet, however, had been busy performing the structural steel subcontract, and its work was completed on time (i.e., on September 30). Faced with the prospect of having to pay the $500,000 contract price (which was due on October 30), Pariah's resorted to the time-honored tactics of professional gamblers, i.e., deceit and subterfuge. Specifically, Pariah's invented all sorts of imagined defects in the steel used by Hot Rivet and the work of Hot Rivet's employees and made repeated, unfounded, and insincere accusations that Hot Rivet was in breach. In short, Pariah's manufactured a dispute with Hot Rivet and threatened to "tie up Hot Rivet in litigation for years," even though Pariah's knew any litigation would be utterly groundless. Then on October 10, Pariah's offered to pay Hot Rivet on October 15 (slightly over two weeks early) and "forget about any law suit" if Hot Rivet would reduce its price to $250,000. Rather than risk litigation, Hot Rivet agreed. However, when October 15 arrived, Pariah's simply did not have the cash to pay Hot Rivet even the reduced price. Indeed, relations between Pariah's and Hot Rivet became so hostile that Hot Rivet was never paid anything at any time.

QUESTIONS

2.   Assume that Sinkhole sues Pariah's for payment for its partial performance of the excavation subcontract. What, if anything, will Sinkhole recover? State the reasons for your answer. (Approximately 45 minutes)

3.   Assuming that Thick Brick had not decided to breach its supply contract with Pariah's, could it have enforced the August 15 modification of the contract? Would your answer be different if the common law of contracts, rather than Article 2 of the Uniform Commercial Code, supplied the governing law? Explain the reasons for your answers. (Approximately 30 minutes)

Given that Thick Brick did repudiate its supply contract, what, if anything, may Pariah's recover for its breach? Would your answer be different if the common law of contracts, rather than Article 2 of the Uniform Commercial Code, supplied the governing law? State the reasons for your answer. (Approximately 30 minutes)

5.   Assume that Hot Rivet sues Pariah's for breach of
      the structural steel subcontract. What, if anything,
      will Hot Rivet recover? State the reasons for your
      answer. (Approximately 45 minutes)

CONTRACTS
ESSAY EXAMS

ANSWERS

CONTRACTS ESSAY EXAM #1

Question #1

I.   ASHCROFT v. BUSCH

   1.   Offer and Acceptance

The conversation between Busch and Ashcroft meets the basic requirements of offer and acceptance for the formation of a bilateral contract. Busch characterizes his proposal as an offer, and Ashcroft's statement, "you have a deal," coupled with a handshake, is an unequivocal acceptance.

   2.   Statute of Frauds

Under the statute of frauds, a contract to transfer an interest in land must be in a writing signed by the party against whom enforcement is sought, and the writing must adequately describe the land. This agreement required a transfer of a portion of Bud Liteacres, and it was never memorialized by a writing. It is therefore arguably unenforceable. However, there are recognized exceptions to the statute of frauds.

   3.   Part Performance Exception to Statute of Frauds

The land clause of the statute of frauds, is subject to a part performance exception. If the vendee under a verbal agreement to transfer an interest in land engages in sufficient partial performance of the agreement, the bar of the statute of frauds may be removed. The basis for the exception is that the conduct in question provides an evidentiary substitute for the writing required by the statute, and that, in the absence of enforcement, the statute of frauds would itself operate as an instrument of fraud.

The difficult question with the part performance exception is determining what type of partial performance is sufficient. Payment of the purchase price, or a portion of it, is not alone sufficient. There must be additional conduct that is "referable" to the agreement in dispute. On the other hand, payment plus taking possession of and making permanent improvements to the land is normally enough. In this case, Ashcroft has made partial payment, but he has not yet taken possession of the agreed portion of Bud Liteacres. He has removed the fence between Ashcroft Acres and Bud Liteacres, and he has dug a ditch on his own side of the original border. The former seems consistent only with the alleged agreement, but the latter is consistent either with the alleged agreement or with a simple desire to improve Ashcroft's own land. It is thus not clear whether a court would find Ashcroft's conduct sufficient to qualify for the partial performance exception.

4.   Specific Performance Remedy

Assuming the partial performance exception to the statute of frauds is applicable to this situation, Ashcroft has the clearest and best remedy. The part performance exception would enable Ashcroft to obtain a decree of specific performance. In order to qualify for specific performance, a litigant must establish that, absent equitable relief, his remedy at law will be inadequate. One form of inadequacy of remedy at law is established if the subject matter of the contract is unique. Each parcel of land is presumed to be unique. Thus, in land sales contracts, specific performance at the request of the vendee is granted almost as a matter of course. There is only one possible obstacle to specific performance. The court must be able to identify the land in question in order to formulate a specific and enforceable decree. While there is no formal legal description of the tract in question in any of the parties' communications, Ashcroft can argue that the measuring and marking of the tract that Busch and Ashcroft performed together is sufficient to enable an equity court to fashion a proper decree. Finally, specific performance will not be ordered if the return performance by the party seeking it is insecure. Therefore, Ashcroft will succeed in obtaining specific performance only if he remains willing and able to pay the remaining $45,000 of the purchase price.

5.　　Promissory Estoppel Exception to the Statute of Frauds

If the part performance exception is not applicable, Ashcroft must find a different way of removing the bar of the statute of frauds. He might try to enforce the agreement on the basis of promissory estoppel, which, in some jurisdictions, may substitute for the writing required by the statute of frauds. Here again, the theory is that the conduct upon which the estoppel is based is a satisfactory evidentiary substitute for the writing and that, unless the defendant is estopped to plead it, the statute of frauds will operate as an instrument of fraud. Liability on the basis of promissory estoppel requires that the defendant make a promise upon which the plaintiff's reliance is reasonably foreseeable, that the plaintiff reasonably rely on the promise, and that injustice be avoidable only through enforcement of the promise. In this case, Busch's offer invited reliance in the form of payment of a portion of the purchase price and excavation of the ditch, and Ashcroft actually relied by doing both. His conduct in removing the fence was not invited, but was arguably foreseeable in view of the contemplated location of the ditch and the subsequent conveyance of the contiguous land. It is therefore arguable that Busch is estopped to plead the statute of frauds.

There are two possible problems with the foregoing analysis. First, the extent to which promissory estoppel is available to remove the bar of the statute of frauds is uncertain as a matter of case law. A general promissory estoppel exception to the statute of frauds has been recommended by the drafters of the Restatement 2d. of Contracts, but not all jurisdictions have adopted the Restatement view. Second, the appropriate remedy in the case of a promise enforceable under an estoppel theory is still controversial. On the one hand, it may be argued that a promise enforceable on the basis of estoppel is, in all other respects, an ordinary contract for the breach of which ordinary contract remedies should be available. If that is the case, specific performance should be available for the reasons outlined above. On the other hand, it is arguable that, if the basis for enforcement is reliance, the available remedy should be limited by the underlying enforcement rationale. In that event, only reliance damages would be available. Ashcroft would be able to recover his down payment, the $5,000 he spent on gasoline etc., plus whatever value could be assigned to his labor.

6. Implied Contract/Quasi Contract

Ashcroft's final option is to pursue recovery under a theory of a contract implied in law. It is well settled that, even if a contract is unenforceable under the statute of frauds, one who confers a benefit on the opposite party in the attempt to perform it may recover in quasi contract for the purpose of preventing unjust enrichment. Thus, Ashcroft could clearly recover the $5,000 portion of the contract price he actually paid. Moreover, one who performs services at the request of another with a known expectation of compensation is entitled to recover the reasonable value of the services performed. Here, it is demonstrable from the offers of other excavation contractors that Ashcroft's services in digging the ditch had a market value of $50,000, and he is presumably entitled to that amount in restitution in addition to restoration of his down payment. Busch might argue that, because the ditch was actually located on Ashcroft Acres, not Bud Liteacres, he had not appropriated the value of the benefit and therefore was not unjustly enriched by Ashcroft's excavation efforts. There are two replies to this argument. First, there is case authority that, where services are performed on request, they are presumed to be of value to the party requesting them equal to their market value, whether that party "appropriates" the results of the services or not. Second, as a matter of fact, the ditch does drain Busch's land, and there is no alternate way, under the facts given, to place a value on that benefit.

Question #2

I. ROSE v. UNCLE BYRD

1. Indefiniteness of promise

The only possible basis for Rose's recovery is the promise contained in the note. Byrd's earlier promise to "see that she did not regret it" if she took care of him was part of a contemporaneous bargain for her services at the time she commenced them, but that promise itself is far too indefinite to give rise to contractual liability.

2. Consideration

The promise in the note to pay Rose $5,000 is sufficiently definite, but it is not supported by classical bargain consideration. In classical cases of consideration, a promise is supported by sufficient consideration if it is part of an exchange and if each side of the exchange induces the other. Here the note recites that its promise to pay money is given in exchange for services that have already been rendered at the time of the promise. The promise thus could not have induced the services. Past consideration, in classical theory, is no consideration, at least where the "past consideration" is something other than a valid legal obligation now barred by a technical defense. Under classical contract law, therefore, the promise in the note would have been unenforceable.

3.   Promise for Benefit Received

In recent cases, the courts have recognized a new basis of recovery on a restitution theory. Where a promisor makes a promise in recognition of a material benefit previously received from the promisee, the promise will be enforced to prevent unjust enrichment, provided circumstances do not establish that the promise was intended as a gift. The justification for the imposition of liability is said to be either (a) that the subsequent promise substitutes for a previous request in establishing that the benefit in question was conferred with the expectation of payment; and/or (b) that the subsequent promise establishes the value the parties placed on the benefit and so liquidates the claim. While some cases in which liability has been imposed do not fit these rationales very well, the case of Uncle Byrd and Rose fits quite well. Services performed by one family member for the benefit of another are normally presumed to be intended as a gratuity. Here that presumption is arguably rebutted both by the subsequent promise to pay $5,000 and the contemporaneous (and admittedly vague) promise that Rose "would not regret it." Moreover, the promise in the note conveniently established the value the promisor placed on the benefit received. In jurisdictions that recognize this line of authority, Rose will have a valid claim for $5,000.

Question #3

I.   LeDough v. Clinton

1.   Objective Theory of Assent

Whether Clinton and LeDough have a contract, and on what terms, is to be determined by application of the objective theory of assent, which requires that the words and conduct of a party be interpreted as a reasonable person would, regardless of the actual subjective intentions of the parties. Clinton's original ad should probably be interpreted, like most advertisements, as a mere invitation to make offers, particularly since it is addressed to the public at large and closes with "send proposals to...." LeDough's e-mail response appears to be an offer, as LeDough characterizes it as a "bid" and purports to incorporate "standard terms." Clinton's e-mail response is by a medium invited by the offer and appears to be an acceptance, as it agrees to the price and specifies a delivery date, as LeDough's offer had requested.

2.   Effect of Misunderstanding

Although both the offer and the acceptance refer to the subject matter of the contract as the "rolls," the two parties attach materially different meanings to the term; Clinton is referring to a car, and LeDough to an order of pastries. In such cases, the objective theory of assent entails the following rules. If neither party knows or has reason to know the meaning of the other, or if both parties know or have reason to know the meaning of the other, there is no contract. There is a simple misunderstanding, and there is no objective reason to prefer one party's interpretation over the other's. In contrast, if one party knows or has reason to know the meaning of the other, but not vice versa, there is a contract on the terms of the innocent (and therefore more reasonable) party. This set of rules is usually traced to the classic case of Raffles v. Wichelhaus (the *Peerless* case) and is reflected in Restatement 2d. of Contracts Section 20.

In this case, it is arguable that Clinton and LeDough each knew or had reason to know the meaning attached to the critical term "rolls" by the other, and that each is therefore equally responsible for the misunderstanding. Clinton, of course, knew from his prior course of dealing with LeDough that LeDough might assume that "rolls" referred to the cinnamon rolls Clinton had ordered on multiple previous occasions and that "standard terms" referred to orders in quantities of 100 for next-day delivery. LeDough's e-mail to Clinton included the name of LeDough's bakery, and Clinton's use of all capitals in his original ad and all small case letters in his e-mail kept him from using the one spelling, "Rolls," that would have put LeDough on notice that a car was intended. On the other hand, LeDough had some reason to suspect that Clinton was referring to a car. LeDough specifically notified Clinton he was going into the used luxury car business by printed announcement, and his own e-mail included not only the name of his bakery but the name of his car dealership. Like Clinton, he used all lower case letters in his e-mail, which helped mask the ambiguity. In short, neither party's interpretation is more reasonable than the other's under the circumstances, and both are responsible for the misunderstanding. Accordingly, there is no contract.

II.   Clinton v. LeDough

    1.   Objective Theory of Assent

Whether Clinton and LeDough have a contract, and on what terms, is to be determined by application of the objective theory of assent, which requires that the words and conduct of a party be interpreted as a reasonable person would, regardless of the actual subjective intentions of the parties. Clinton's original ad should probably be interpreted, like most advertisements, as a mere invitation to make offers, particularly since it is addressed to the public at large and closes with "send proposals to...." LeDough's e-mail response appears to be an offer, as LeDough characterizes it as a "bid" and purports to incorporate "standard terms." Clinton's e-mail response is by a medium invited by the offer and appears to be an acceptance, as it agrees to the price and specifies a delivery date, as LeDough's offer had requested.

2.   Effect of Misunderstanding

Although both the offer and the acceptance refer to the subject matter of the contract as the "rolls," the two parties attach materially different meanings to the term; Clinton is referring to a car, and LeDough to an order of pastries.   In such cases, the objective theory of assent entails the following rules. If neither party knows or has reason to know the meaning of the other, or if both parties know or have reason to know the meaning of the other, there is no contract.   There is a simple misunderstanding, and there is no objective reason to prefer one party's interpretation over the other's.   In contrast, if one party knows or has reason to know the meaning of the other, but not vice versa, there is a contract on the terms of the innocent (and therefore more reasonable) party. This set of rules is usually traced to the classic case of Raffles v. Wichelhaus (the *Peerless* case) and is reflected in Restatement 2d. of Contracts Section 20.

In this case, it is arguable that Clinton and LeDough each knew or had reason to know the meaning attached to the critical term "rolls" by the other, and that each is therefore equally responsible for the misunderstanding.   Clinton, of course, knew from his prior course of dealing with LeDough that LeDough might assume that "rolls" referred to the cinnamon rolls Clinton had ordered on multiple previous occasions and that "standard terms" referred to orders in quantities of 100 for next-day delivery.   LeDough's e-mail to Clinton included the name of LeDough's bakery, and Clinton's use of all capitals in his original ad and all small case letters in his e-mail kept him from using the one spelling, "Rolls," that would have put LeDough on notice that a car was intended.   On the other hand, LeDough had some reason to suspect that Clinton was referring to a car. LeDough specifically notified Clinton he was going into the used luxury car business by printed announcement, and his own e-mail included not only the name of his bakery but the name of his car dealership. Like Clinton, he used all lower case letters in his e-mail, which helped mask the ambiguity. In short, neither party's interpretation is more reasonable than the other's under the circumstances, and both are responsible for the misunderstanding. Accordingly, there is no contract.

Question #4

I.   LeDough v. Clinton

    1.   Damage Remedies

If there had been a contract for cinnamon rolls, Clinton would have been in breach and LeDough would have the remedies of an aggrieved seller under Article 2 of the U.C.C., which governs sales of goods. Since the cinnamon rolls tendered to Clinton were put in inventory and sold, it is conceivable that LeDough could be regarded as a seller resorting to his resale remedy under 2-706. However, since it is not clear which buyer bought "Clinton's" rolls, it is better to analyze the case under the market price differential formula of 2-708. LeDough is entitled under 2-708(1) to the difference between contract price ($2.20) and market price (which remained at $2.20) times the contract quantity (100) (plus incidental and consequential damages and less expenses saved as a result of the breach, none of which are present in this case). This yields a zero recovery. 2-708(2) provides that, if the formula of 2-708(1) is inadequate to put the seller in as good a position as full performance, he may recover lost profits. This provides an expectancy recovery to a lost volume seller in situations in which the market price of the goods at issue has not changed. Is LeDough a lost volume seller? The facts do not provide a definitive answer. If LeDough could have made more cinnamon rolls even if Clinton had accepted 100, so that his sales to *other* customers would have been the same if Clinton had not breached, LeDough qualifies as a lost volume seller and can recover $20 in lost profits from Clinton ($220 total price less $200 cost to produce). If, on the other hand, LeDough's total possible supply for the day included the 100 designated for Clinton, so that Clinton's breach enabled him to sell that 100 to another customer, Clinton can argue successfully that LeDough's sale to another customer and exhaustion of his total supply effectively mitigated any damages.

Question #5

I. Clinton v LeDough

  1. Damage Remedies

If the contract was for a sale of a car, LeDough has breached by failure to deliver. Since Clinton has not covered, 2-712 is inapplicable and 2-713 determines damages. Clinton is entitled to market price at the time he learned of the breach less contract price (plus incidental and consequential damages and less expenses saved as a result of the breach, none of which are present in this case). The phrase, "the time the buyer learned of the breach" found in 2-713(1), creates no interpretive difficulties in this case because it is not a case of anticipatory repudiation but rather a case of simple failure to deliver. Clinton learned of the breach on the date performance was due and was not forthcoming, December 5. The market price on that day, however, is difficult to ascertain because the market for used Rolls Royces is so thin. The usual market price seems to be wholesale cost plus 20%. Clinton's contract price was cost plus 10%, so the damages should be the difference of 10% of wholesale cost. However, in the relevant time period, wholesale cost in the relevant market varied from a low of $40,000 to a high of $60,000. This means Clinton's damages could be as low as $4,000 or as high as $6,000. Given the thin market, it is difficult to specify one figure as "the" market price on December 5. A court could respond in one of two possible ways. Some courts might deny recovery altogether, on the theory that the expectancy was speculative. Other courts might follow the "least level of benefit rule" and award Clinton the minimum benefit he could have received under the contract, i.e., an expectancy of $4,000.

CONTRACTS ESSAY EXAM #2

Question #1

I.   KISSINGER v. BUSH

1.   Unilateral v. Bilateral Contract Distinction

Before addressing the issue of enforceability, it is necessary to classify the agreement as unilateral or bilateral. In making such a determination, the words and actions of the parties are to be assessed under the objective theory of assent—i.e., they are to be interpreted as a reasonable person would interpret them. George W's statement, "I want you to commit now for the full fifteen months so I don't have to worry about this any more," followed closely by "What do you say?" compels the conclusion that he was making an offer of a bilateral contract. Kissinger's affirmative response during the same telephone conversation would normally suffice as an acceptance of the offer.

2.   Contract for Specific Term vs. Employment at Will

Interpreting George W's offer as a reasonable person would, it is clear that the agreement was for a definite term of fifteen months. George W did not use vague expressions such as "permanent" or "lifetime" employment that might be construed restrictively to refer to employment at will, which is at least capable of completion within a year. Rather, he referred to "constant tutoring from now through December 2000," specified an "absolute minimum of fifteen months," and emphasized "no more, no less."

3.   Statute of Frauds

As the agreement was not capable of being performed within the space of one year, the statute of frauds required it to be in writing. However, all the communications between the parties that might otherwise have created a contract were verbal statements during the course of a telephone conversation. The agreement therefore violates the statute of frauds and is unenforceable. Kissinger might try to argue that the George W's statements created a standing offer for a series of unilateral contracts, each with a duration of one month, which he (Kissinger) accepted each time he actually gave a tutorial. If accepted, such an argument would establish the existence of 3 unilateral contracts (for October, November, and December), none of which violated the statute of frauds. However, the argument is too weak to be accepted, in light of the language George W actually used.

Question #2

I.   Kissinger v. Bush

1.   Expectation Damages

Assuming the agreement had been enforceable, George W's telegram would be an anticipatory repudiation. The normal remedy for breach of an enforceable contract is an award of expectancy damages, an amount sufficient to put the aggrieved party in as good a position as full performance. Here the obvious measure of the expectancy is the full salary for the fifteen month term of the contract, $5,000 per month X 15 months = $75,000.

2.   Duty to Mitigate

Kissinger would be under a duty to mitigate damages, which means that his damage award would be subject to reduction by the amount of any loss he could have avoided through reasonable effort and the amount of any gain made possible by the breach. The burden of establishing the amount of the reduction dictated by the avoidability principle would be on the breaching defendant, George W, and it is unlikely he could meet that burden in this case. Kissinger's services are no longer in demand, and it is thus unlikely that alternative employment is available to him for purposes of mitigating damages. Even if alternate employment were available to Kissinger, George W has virtually admitted that his own tutoring sessions take up so little of Kissinger's time that Kissinger could work for others at the same time. It is thus unlikely that any gains Kissinger realizes in the future would be made possible by the breach and so applied in mitigation of damages.

Question #3

I.   Kissinger v. Bush

1.   Promissory Estoppel

Assuming that the agreement is unenforceable due to the statute of frauds, the remedial issues become more complicated. Initially, Kissinger might attempt to save the agreement from invalidation by arguing that the theory of promissory estoppel may be invoked to remove the barrier of the statute of frauds. Kissinger's argument would be that he reasonably and foreseeably relied upon George W's promise of employment, and that injustice may only be avoided by enforcing the contract notwithstanding the violation of the statute of frauds. George W has at least two counterarguments.

The use of promissory estoppel as a device to circumvent the statute of frauds is itself controversial. Its supporters argue that reliance is a satisfactory evidentiary substitute for the writing otherwise required by the statute of frauds and that, absent recognition of a promissory estoppel exception, the statute of frauds itself may become an instrument of fraud. These arguments have been found persuasive by some courts as well as the drafters of Restatement 2d. 139. However, other courts have found that, in the employment context, the sort of reliance that is usually alleged—foregoing other opportunities and performing the alleged agreement—is not sufficiently reliable as an evidentiary substitute for a writing. Such courts refuse to recognize the exception altogether or, at least, impose a heightened evidentiary burden on the party asserting the estoppel theory, effectively requiring proof of reliance so substantial that refusal of enforcement would amount to tolerance of fraud. It is doubtful that Kissinger could meet such a heightened burden of proof. He was not required to forego other opportunities to work for Bush. His time commitment was minimal, and he incurred no out-of-pocket expenditures.

2.   Measure of Damages

The measure of damages in promissory estoppel cases is still controversial. Most courts apply an expectancy measure where it is possible to do so. That practice is supported by the argument that estoppel is merely a substitute for some normal element of a contract—often consideration but here the requirement of a writing. In other respects, promises enforced under a theory of estoppel are not significantly different from ordinary contracts and should be enforced the same way, by an award of expectancy damages. On the other hand, it is arguable that, if reliance supplies the ground of enforcement, the remedy should go no further than the enforcement rationale, and damages should be confined to the reliance measure. As indicated above, Kissinger has incurred no out of pocket or opportunity costs, and the value of his lost time and effort will be controversial.

3,   Quantum Meruit

Even if Kissinger's estoppel theory fails, it is well-established that he has a right to sue in quantum meruit for the value of the services rendered in his attempt to perform the agreement barred by the statute of frauds. George W might argue that he has not been unjustly enriched as Kissinger has conferred no direct financial benefit upon him analogous to the payment of a sum of money. However, this argument will probably be rejected. When services are rendered at the request of one party and the services are either normally compensated or actually performed with a known expectation of compensation, the services are presumed to be of value to the requesting party, and the law will imply a promise to pay the reasonable value of such services.

While Kissinger's right to recover in quasi-contract is clear, the measure of recovery may generate some controversy. Since Kissinger is suing "off" the unenforceable agreement, the contract price for the services ($5,000 per month) is not necessarily decisive. However, a court might regard the specified rate as an admission by the parties of what the tutoring services are worth and award Kissinger $15,000 for the completion of three months' work. On the other hand, the value of such services in the market is substantially less. Kissinger knows it to be around $2,000 per month, and a court therefore might confine his restitution recovery to $6,000.

Question #4

I.   Hillary v. The Donald

1.   Good Faith Modification of Contracts

Since Hillary has been paid the original contract price, she only has a remedy against the Donald if the modification of the price to $20 per dozen is enforceable. Under 2-209(1), an agreement modifying a contract for the sale of goods needs no consideration to be binding. Comment 2 to 2-209 indicates that modification agreements are to be policed by a requirement of good faith. The same Comment suggests that extortion of a modification without legitimate commercial reason is barred, but that a market shift which makes one party's performance possible only at a loss might be such a legitimate reason. In this case there was a sudden, dramatic increase in Hillary's raw material costs, and the modification she sought was no more than necessary for her to break even. This undoubtedly meets the test of good faith, and Hillary may collect the additional $10 per dozen, for a total of $3,000.

2.   Pre-Existing Duty Rule

Under the common law, the analysis would have been different, although the outcome might have been the same under more modern lines of case authority. Under classical common law rules, the modification would have been unenforceable. The pre-existing duty rule requires a modification to be supported by fresh consideration. Promising to do, or actually doing, what one is previously legally obligated to do does not qualify as consideration. In this case, Hillary merely promised to do what she was already obligated to do—deliver 300 dozen cookies—in return for a promise of a price increase.

3.   Rescission and Novation

The common law courts evolved a variety of legal theories to mitigate the harshness of the pre-existing duty rule, some of which might apply to this case. Because the duties of both Hillary and the Donald were executory at the time they agreed to the price increase, Hillary could argue that she and the Donald were "really" rescinding the old agreement and entering into an entirely new one at the higher price. However, the rescission and novation theory has no real factual support here.

4.   Unforeseen Circumstances Exception to Pre-existing Duty Rule

The "unforeseen circumstances" exception to the pre-existing duty rule might be more promising. Recent cases, originating in the context of construction contracts, have permitted the enforcement of one-sided modifications if the modification in question is fair and equitable in light of circumstances unforeseen at the time of contracting that make the performance of one party under the original contract substantially more onerous than the parties contemplated. The Drafters of the Restatement 2d. of Contracts Section 89 recommend the unforeseen circumstances exception as a rule even outside the construction context. In this case, the requirements of the exception appear to be satisfied. While some degree of volatility in the market price of sugar may always be foreseeable, both the source and degree of the spike in the price of Hillary's raw materials probably were not. The resulting increase in her cost of performance was onerous—it threatened her business with bankruptcy. Moreover, the adjustment seems fair and equitable, as Hillary sought no greater price increase than was necessary to break even on her performance. Assuming the unforeseen circumstances exception is generalizable beyond the construction context that generated it, it probably saves the price modification. If so, Hillary recovers an additional $3,000 from the Donald.

Question #5

I.   The Donald v. Hillary

1.   UCC Cover Remedy

Under UCC Article 2-712, the Donald has a right (though not a duty) to obtain commercially reasonable cover in good faith and within a reasonable time and recover the difference between cover price and contract price, plus incidental and consequential damages, less expenses saved as a result of the breach. The Donald arranged a cover transaction very quickly with the only available source of supply. Comment 2 to 2-712 suggests that the fact that the Donald paid a premium over the normal price of a forward contract does not make his cover transaction unreasonable. All the normal sources of supply were already committed elsewhere when the Donald's need for cover arose, and his purchase from Heston of goods that are not precisely identical with those specified in the original contract is likewise permitted by Comment 2. So the Donald will recover the excess of cover price ($30 per dozen) over contract price ($20 per dozen) or $10, multiplied by the contract quantity (300 dozen) for a total of $3,000.

2.   Consequential Damages under UCC

The Donald's payment of $50,000 in settlement of the hotel's claim is not recoverable from Hillary as consequential damages, whether it is analyzed as an ordinary consequential damage claim under 2-715(2)(a) or as a property damage claim under 2-715(2)(b). (2)(a) incorporates the common law rule of Hadley v. Baxendale by specifying that consequential loss must result from "general or particular requirements and needs of which the seller at the time contracting had reason to know." Damages due to physical violence by agitated activists are not a normal consequence of the breach of contracts for cookies, and Hillary had no specific reason to expect it. (2)(b) incorporates a requirement of proximate cause for property damage claims, and the chain of proximate causation is probably broken by the either the bizarre actions of the activists, Heston's design of the substitute goods, or perhaps Donald's own action in settling the claim.

3.   Common Law Damage Remedies

When the seller's breach of a sale contract took the form of an anticipatory repudiation, the common law was somewhat less favorable to **cover transactions** by the buyer. In particular, if cover price turned out to be higher than the market price on the date fixed for delivery, the common law would measure damages by the difference between market price and contract price, rather than cover price and contract price. The common law courts reasoned that the premium over market price was avoidable, as there was no duty to cover. The drafters of Article 2 included 2-712 in order to change the common law rule. However, this is not a case of anticipatory repudiation but a case of breach on the date fixed for performance. The price of a forward contract at an earlier time is irrelevant, and there really is no market price on the date the breach occurred, since cookies are unavailable from ordinary suppliers. Measuring expectancy damages using the cover price would appear to be the only alternative even under common law rules.

The **foreseeabilty** and **proximate cause** limitations of 2-715(2)(a) and (b) are actually derived from common law rules.

CONTRACTS ESSAY EXAM #3

Question #1

I.   Reno v. Stone

1.   Statute of Frauds

The statute of frauds is no barrier to enforcement of the contract. While the agreement between Janet and Hart was verbal, it was a service contract with a specified maximum term of three months. The statute of frauds only requires a writing if a contract for services involves services that are not to be performed within a year.

2.   Specific Performance

A suit for specific performance of the contract would not succeed. The general presumption is that the breach of a contract creates an action for damages, not for specific relief. Specific performance may be awarded if the remedy at law (i.e., an action for damages) is inadequate for some reason. Uniqueness of subject matter is one such reason, but it is doubtful Hart's services are in any sense unique. He is one of a number of mediocre artists, and substitutes for him are readily available.

Moreover, there is a general presumption against an award of specific performance in the case of contracts for services. The presumption rests on a general policy against involuntary servitude, a disinclination to force the continuation of relationships that have already soured, and the administrative difficulties created by the need to monitor the quality of an ongoing contractual performance. While, in rare instances, courts grant specific performance if the breaching party's services are so exceptional that there simply is no possible substitute,

Hart's services are not sufficiently unique to overcome the presumption.

II.   Stone v. Reno

1.   Restitution Recovery

Hart has breached the contract, but he has also performed half of the work it required. The question is therefore whether the party in breach may recover for the value of the portion of the contract he has performed. At one time, even restitution recovery was not available to a party in breach. While restitution recovery has been liberalized, it is still, in some jurisdictions, denied to a party who has committed a willful breach. If California is such a jurisdiction, Hart will only be able to recover if his breach was not "willful." There is, however, some ambiguity in the standard of "willfulness." "Willful" might be interpreted to mean "deliberate," so that only plaintiffs who breached unintentionally or who were unable to perform completely could recover for partial performance. Such a standard would preclude Hart's recovery, as his breach was neither inadvertent nor compelled. On the other hand, "willful" might be interpreted to mean "malicious," and it seems doubtful that Hart's breach was motivated by actual malice.

2.   Offset to Restitution Recovery

In some jurisdictions, however, even a willfully breaching plaintiff may recover for the reasonable value of the work he has performed. His recovery is, however, subject to an offset in the amount of the expectancy loss that his breach caused the innocent party to sustain. In this case Hart performed half the required work. The facts suggest that the contract price of $10,000 reflected the market rate for comparable services, and the reasonable value of Hart's performance is thus probably $5,000. However, assuming Janet accepted Sandy's offer to complete the statue, and that she was reasonable in doing so, the second half of the work cost her $6,000, rather than the $5,000 she would have had to pay Hart. Accordingly, she sustained an expectancy loss of $1,000 that must be deducted from Hart's recovery. Hart's maximum recovery is therefore $4,000.

Question #3

I. Stephanopoulos v. Reno

1. Revocability of Offers

Janet's written offer to George remained revocable at will, notwithstanding the express commitment to hold it open. It was not an option contract, as George paid no consideration for the promise not to revoke. Even under the more liberal standards of the Restatement 2d 87(1), which requires only a recitation of consideration for a commitment to irrevocability, Janet's offer remains revocable because it contained no such recitation. The commitment to hold the offer open until April 30 was thus gratuitous and unenforceable.

2. Mailbox Rule

Janet's revocation came too late. Under the mailbox rule, an acceptance is effective upon proper dispatch. George dispatched his acceptance by the very means Janet had designated on April 5. Janet's "revocation" was not even dispatched until April 6 and could not have been effective until its receipt on April 20. George thus exercised his power of acceptance and formed a valid contract on April 5, and Janet's purported revocation was actually a breach by repudiation.

3. Expectation Damages

George is entitled to recover expectation damages from Janet. He should be awarded an amount sufficient to put him in as good a position as he would have occupied had Janet performed as promised. In this case, the value of George's expectancy consists of the promised $30,000 salary plus the value of whatever health insurance benefits are standard in the Encino labor market.

4.   Duty to Mitigate

However, the mitigation principle requires reduction of George's recovery by whatever amount George earned, or could have earned through reasonable efforts, because he was not required to perform his contract with Janet. Employment as a male stripper is probably different in kind and inferior in quality to employment as a MAGGOTT, and Janet could not have reduced George's recovery for failure to mitigate had he declined to accept the job at Chippendale's. However, George did accept it, and, because both the Chippendale's job and Janet's job involved work on the night shift, George could not have held both jobs. Accordingly, George's earnings from Chippendale's were made possible by the breach and must be deducted from his recovery. He therefore recovers $10,000 plus the value of the health insurance benefits Janet promised (assuming Chippendale's provides no such benefits).

5.   Indefiniteness

George is not entitled to any additional expectancy recovery for the contemplated renewal of his agreement with Janet. A commitment to renew the contract "on whatever terms are acceptable to both of us" is a mere agreement to agree and is too indefinite to be enforced.

Question #4

I.   Reno v. Hudson Foods

1.   Cover Remedy

The contract between Janet and Hudson is a sale of goods governed by Article 2 of the UCC. Hudson, the seller, has breached by failure to deliver. Under 2-711, Janet was entitled to exercise her right to cover under 2-712. 2-712 requires that Janet cover in good faith, within a commercially reasonable time and on commercially reasonable terms. She appears to have done so, as her cover contract with Jagged Claw was made within a day at the prevailing market price. Moreover, Jagged Claw appears to have offered the speediest delivery, which was important for purposes of minimizing Janet's lost profits. Accordingly, Janet's direct damages are measured by cover price ($2.00 per pound) minus contract price ($1.00 per pound), multiplied by the contract quantity (10,000 pounds) for a total of $10,000. At a minimum, Janet is entitled to that amount.

2. Foreseeability Requirement

Janet's potential consequential losses include her lost pension benefits and her lost opening night profits. The former are clearly precluded by the foreseeability requirement of *Hadley v. Baxendale,* which has been codified at 2-715(2)(a). That section limits consequential damages to those resulting from the general or particular requirements of the buyer that the seller, at the time of contracting, had reason to know. The loss of pension benefits due to the intervening act of a vindictive, hungry President is not foreseeable under either branch of the *Hadley* test. Janet's lost profits recovery, however, is not precluded by the *Hadley* rule. Comment 6 to 2-715 indicates that a seller of goods to one in the business of reselling them should always foresee that a breach will result in lost profits, and Comment 6 probably extends to cases (like Janet's) in which the buyer minimally processes the goods shortly before resale.

3. Speculative Damages and New Business Rule

However, Janet's claim for loss of her opening night profits may be too speculative to be recoverable. Clearly, in a jurisdiction that followed the traditional "new business rule", the lost profits of a brand new business like Planet Janet would be too speculative as a matter of law. Even in a jurisdiction that did not follow the new business rule, a court might conclude that the profits of the opening night of a new venture are subject to so many unpredictable and unprovable variables that evidence of lost profits must be kept from the trier of fact. However, Janet does have evidence of the average daily profits for both an inferior local restaurant and a comparable but well-established local restaurant, and it is conceivable that a court following the modern trend might allow the evidence to go to the jury.

Question #5

I.   Edwards v. Reno

1.   Modification of Contracts

Edwin has no rights and remedies against Janet. Janet has paid Edwin all that is due under the original contract, and the modification of the contract to increase his salary is not enforceable.

2.   Defense of Duress

Initially, there is a possible argument that Edwin obtained the modification through economic duress. In order to establish duress, Janet would be required to show that Edwin obtained her agreement by making a wrongful threat that left her no reasonable alternative but to acquiesce. Since a substitute MAGGOTT was unavailable, Edwin's threat arguably left Janet no reasonable alternative (or, in the language of older cases, it was "sufficient to overcome her free will"). In some jurisdictions, the requirement of an improper threat might be met by Edwin's threat to repudiate. However, in other jurisdictions there are still cases clinging to the older rules that the actions threatened must be more than a breach of contract, or even be criminal, in order to constitute duress. In those jurisdictions, the defense of duress would not succeed.

3.   Pre-existing Duty Rule

Janet has a better argument that the modification is unenforceable under the pre-existing duty rule. Edwin has promised to do no more than perform the services he was already obligated to perform under his original contract with Janet, and such a promise is not consideration for her return promise to increase his salary.

4.   Surrender of Claim as Consideration

The pre-existing duty rule is not violated if, in addition to promising to perform his pre-existing duty, Edwin is surrendering a legitimately disputed claim. However, in order to qualify as consideration, the claim surrendered must be one that the party surrendering believes, in good faith, to be valid, and in many jurisdictions it must also have some arguable objective basis.   The claim that health insurance benefits are inadequate if they do not cover crawfish etouffe is so laughable that it is clearly without objective basis, and its absurdity makes it unlikely that Edwin even has a good faith belief in its validity.   The settlement of Edwin's "claim" for breach of the contract to provide health insurance thus cannot supply the consideration necessary to support the modification of his salary.

5.   Exceptions to Pre-existing Duty Rule

None of the judicially created exceptions to the pre-existing duty rule are applicable to this situation. There is no evidentiary basis for characterizing the modification (i.e., the salary increase) as a mutual rescission of the original contract and the formation of an entirely new contract. Likewise, it is impossible to characterize a salary increase as a permissible gratuitous "waiver" of a known right. Under the modern trend of authority, an otherwise gratuitous modification may be enforced if it is fair and equitable in light of circumstances not foreseen at the time of contracting that make one party's performance substantially more onerous. However, there are no unforeseen circumstances making Edwin's performance substantially more onerous, and so there is no basis for invoking the unforeseen circumstances exception. Janet's promise to raise Edwin's salary therefore fails the test of the pre-existing duty rule. As Edwin has received all that is due under the original contract, he has no rights against Janet.

CONTRACTS ESSAY EXAM #4

Question #1

I.   Clinton v. Fatcatt

1.   Sufficiency of Consideration

Is Fatcatt's promise supported by consideration or some substitute for it? Bill may argue that the promise was supported by consideration because he offered Fatcatt inducements (the mug, the umbrella, etc.) in order to pledge, and the courts do not examine the adequacy of consideration. This argument will fail. In order to be supported by consideration, a promise must be given in exchange for a return promise or performance, and the return promise or performance must induce, and be induced by, the promise at issue. While lop-sided exchanges are indeed permissible, the problem in this case is that Fatcatt's promise was not induced by the premiums Bill offered, notwithstanding Bill's characterization of them as "incentives." Bill also characterized them as "free gifts," and Fatcatt made it clear that he did not even want them ("Keep your trinkets").   Therefore, consideration in the classical sense is absent.

Nor is there any recitation in the pledge card that would provide a predicate for the fallacious and fictitious theories of consideration that the courts have occasionally used to sustain charitable subscriptions. For example, there is no recitation that the pledge of $20,000 was given in exchange for the continuation of charitable work or the similar subscriptions of others.

2.   Promissory Estoppel

Since there is no consideration, Bill's next argument would be that the promise may be enforced on a theory of promissory estoppel, which permits enforcement on the basis that reasonable and foreseeable reliance provides a substitute for consideration. Promissory estoppel requires a promise that the promisor should reasonably expect to induce reliance, actual reasonable reliance by the promisee, and a finding that injustice can only be avoided by enforcement of the promise. It is clear that the pledge is a promise. It is also clear that Bill incurred substantial expenditures and liabilities in reliance on the entire set of pledges he obtained. Some of that reliance (e.g., the golf membership and the Scotch) may not have been foreseeable or reasonable, but other expenditures and liabilities (the lease, the secretary, the lawyer) were both foreseeable and reasonable. The chief obstacle to the promissory estoppel theory, however, is that is impossible to identify any specific act of reliance that was induced by Fatcatt's promise in particular. His pledge was not earmarked for any specific purpose, and so pairing it with any particular act of reliance would be arbitrary. If the theory of promissory estoppel is applied strictly, therefore, Bill's argument fails.

The case thus presents directly the question whether charitable subscriptions are enforceable even in the absence of consideration or actual particular reliance. Restatement (Second) of Contracts Section 90(2) recommends such enforcement, but there is a conflict of authority on the point. It has been argued that such promises should be enforceable on the basis of public policy, particularly where, as here, the promisor is alive and the promise is in writing, thus satisfying cautionary, evidentiary and channeling concerns.

Question #2

I.   Roger v. Bill

   1.   Statute of Frauds

The action on a ten-year contract will fail. Initially, even if Bill and Roger did agree to a contract with a ten-year term, the contract would be unenforceable under the statute of frauds. The statute requires a writing for any contract that is not to be performed within a year, and Bill and Roger never executed a writing.

2.   Objective Theory of Assent

Even if Bill and Roger do have an employment contract of some kind, it is is necessary to determine the duration of the employment that Bill promised Roger.. The only statements that address the issue of the contract's duration are Bill's rather vague responses to Roger's question, "How long will it last?"   Under the objective theory of assent, Bill's responses are to be given the interpretation that a reasonable person would give them.

3.   Contract for Definite Term vs. Employment at Will

The issue to be resolved under the objective theory of assent is whether Bill promised Roger employment for a specific term of term years or only indefinite employment, terminable at will be either party. Roger's only possible argument that Bill committed to a minimum ten-year term would be based on the facts that (a) Bill's statements were made in response to a specific question of obvious importance to Roger; (b) the specific mention of ten years; (c) the invitation to trust Bill ("Trust me...I'll take care of you.") Bill, however, probably has a stronger counterargument.   Some of his reassurances ("Trust me...I'll take care of you.") are really too vague to be promises of anything in particular.   Others are too tentative or qualified ("Who knows? Maybe ten years, maybe forever.   Maybe you'll die tomorrow.") Most importantly, Bill specifically characterized the proffered employment as "permanent." The traditional common law rule is that an offer of permanent employment is construed as an offer of indefinite employment, terminable at the will of either party. There is an exception if the employee provides specific consideration for an employer's promise of employment on other terms (e.g., employment for life or discharge subject to a requirement of good cause), but Roger supplied no such promise-specific consideration. Therefore, even if Bill and Roger had a contract, it was a contract for employment terminable at will.

4. Mirror Image Rule

Bill might argue that he and Roger had no contract at all. Under the common law mirror image rule, his initial offer of employment at $2,000 per month was rejected when Roger stated "I will need $3,000 a month...$2 000 is not enough." At best, that deviant response was a counteroffer. Given the sequence of communications, it is probably most reasonable to construe Roger's statement as a counteroffer at $3,000 a month, incorporating Bill's representations concerning duration. That counteroffer would indeed operate to reject Bill's initial offer. Bill's reply, however, ("$3,000 a month it is. Welcome aboard.") is most reasonably interpreted as an acceptance of the counteroffer, and thus Bill cannot prevail entirely on his claim that no contract was formed.

5. Reliance-based Damages

Bill could argue that the expectancy on a contract terminable at will is too speculative to be awarded. Alternatively, he could argue that the unlimited termination right implicit in at will employment implies that such a contract effectively cannot be breached except as to performance already rendered. Either argument might be accepted. However, there is authority that, where a contract terminable at will is breached by anticipatory repudiation, damages measured by the reliance interest may be awarded, at least if the elements of promissory estoppel are satisfied.   Those elements seem to be present in this case.   Bill knew of Roger's job with the Dew Drop Inn because Roger told him about it during negotiations.   Bill thus had reason to anticipate Roger might rely on his promise of employment by terminating his former employment, assuming Roger could not have held both jobs at once.   On the same assumption, Roger's resignation appears to be both reasonable and causally related to the contract with Bill. It is thus at least arguably appropriate to award Roger the $48,000 guaranteed salary he gave up by relying on Bill's promise of employment.   Roger appears to have satisfied his duty to mitigate damages by seeking employment either in his former capacity or the capacity promised by Bill.

Question #3(a)

I.   Lamar v. Clinton

1.   Revocability of Offers

At common law, an offeror could revoke an offer at any time, even in spite of assurances it would be held open, in the absence of consideration for a period of irrevocability.   An offer was conceived as a conditional promise or set of promises, and, like any other promise, it was unenforceable in the absence of Consideration.   No consideration was provided for the offer at issue in this case.

2.   UCC Firm Offers

However, the contract at issue is a sale of goods governed by Article 2 of the U.C.C.   2-205 specifically permits a merchant offeror to make an irrevocable offer on the basis of form rather than consideration.   The elements of 2-205 are satisfied.   Bill is a dealer in goods of the kind and so qualifies as a merchant.   (2-104(1)). The offer is written and signed, and it contains an express assurance that it will be held open until a date certain. The maximum three month period of irrevocability is not exceeded. Accordingly, Bill's attempted revocation on March 7 is ineffective. Lamar accepted by the means designated within the period of irrevocability. A contract was formed, and Bill is in breach.

Question #3(b)

I.   Lamar v. Clinton

1.   Cover Remedy

Because Lamar chose to cover, his recovery is measured by 2-712. Bill's attempted "revocation" amounts to an anticipatory repudiation. Lamar's initial response was an attempt to persuade Bill to perform, which 2-610 permits. Lamar then covered by buying from Jimmy. Because Jimmy's price is standard and thus would not appear to fluctuate, waiting until March 20 would appear reasonable. Jimmy's product also appears to be the only reasonable substitute for Bill's, and the terms of the sale (and specifically the price) appear to be the only ones Jimmy will agree to. Lamar's cover therefore appears to be within a reasonable time and on reasonable terms. Damages are therefore the cover price ($3.00 per bottle) minus the contract price ($2.00 per bottle), multiplied by the contract quantity (1000) for a total of $1,000. (There are no facts suggesting incidental damages, consequential damages, or expenses saved by virtue of the breach.)

Question #4

I.   Clinton v. Ferdinand

1.   Market Price Differential Damages

Bill is a seller of goods faced with repudiation by a buyer, and his potential damage remedies are found in 2-

706 (in the event he sells the goods subject to the contract) or 2-708 (in the event he does not). Because Bill cannot now identify the goods subject to the contract with Ferdinand, it is difficult to see how his subsequent transactions could be considered resales under 2-706. Accordingly, it is best to analyze the problem under 2-708. The basic market price differential measure of damages is provided in 2-708(1). Damages consist of the contract price minus the market price at the time and place for tender, plus incidental damages and less expenses saved by virtue of the breach. (Again there is no indication of incidental damages or expenses saved.) Because Bill is selling standard priced goods, this measure yields a zero recovery. Bill's "market price" is the same as the contract price, i.e. $2.50.

2. Lost Volume Seller Damages

Bill is apparently a lost volume seller. He apparently can produce all the goods he needs to satisfy demand, and, had the contract been performed, his total sales volume would have been 100 bottles higher. His actual loss is therefore the lost profit on 100 bottles. Since his cost is $1.00 per bottle and his selling price is $2.50 per bottle, his total lost profit is $150.00. 2-708(2) authorizes recovery of lost profits if 2-708(1) is inadequate to put the aggrieved seller in as good a position as full performance. Bill is in exactly that position, and Comment 2 to 2-708 establishes a presumption that 2-708(2) applies to all contracts for standard priced goods. Accordingly, Bill may recover the $150.00 in lost profits from Ferdinand.

CONTRACTS ESSAY EXAM #5

Question #1

I.   New Babylon v. McDonald

1.   Revocability of Offers

The first issue is whether or not McDonald and New Babylon formed a contract. The offer of June 1 was fully revocable. New Babylon paid no consideration for a period of irrevocability, and, under the objective theory of assent, the final sentence of the quoted paragraph probably is a mere specification of a lapse date, not a commitment to make the offer irrevocable.

2.   Offer and Acceptance and Mailbox Rule

However, the dispositive issue is whether McDonald revoked the offer prior to its acceptance. Under the common law mailbox rule, an acceptance of an offer is effective upon proper dispatch. McDonald's statement that the city "must accept by June 10" is probably not sufficiently unequivocal to negate the mailbox rule under the objective theory of assent. Klutz deposited New Babylon's acceptance letter in the mail on June 8, and the letter had a correct address and proper postage. The acceptance was therefore effective on June 8, before the offer either expired by its own terms or was revoked. McDonald's telegram of June 9 was therefore ineffective as a revocation. A contract had already been formed on June 8.

3.   Statute of Frauds

The statute of frauds requires that a contract for the transfer of an interest in land be evidenced by a writing signed by the party to be charged. In this case, however, the contract is not rendered unenforceable by the statute of frauds because McDonald's original offer was contained in a signed writing sufficient to satisfy the statute of frauds. The land clause of the statute of frauds is generally interpreted fairly strictly, and courts often require that the writing contain a description of the land at issue. Again however, McDonald's offer meets this requirement. McDonald's refusal to convey the farm is a breach.

4.   Specific Performance

The final question is whether or not the city is entitled to specific performance. A plaintiff seeking equitable relief must initially demonstrate that his remedy at law is inadequate. If the subject matter of a contract is unique, however, the normal legal remedy—an award of damages—is inadequate. Each parcel of land is presumed to be unique, and the city therefore should have no difficulty meeting the threshold condition for specific performance. There is no discretionary ground for refusing equitable relief, as no personal services are involved and the city's own performance is not insecure. Specific relief should therefore be granted.

Question #2

I.   Sinkhole v. Pariah's

1.   Restitution

The initial issue is whether Sinkhole can recover for partial performance of its contract notwithstanding its own breach. The general rule is that a plaintiff in breach of a contract may recover in restitution the reasonable value of his partial performance, less any damage his breach has caused the innocent party. In some jurisdictions, such a restitution recovery is denied a plaintiff whose breach of the subject contract was willful. Even if Disarray is such a jurisdiction, however, there was nothing willful about Sinkhole's breach. Sinkhole breached because it was unable to perform, and its inability was a result of a fire and its own lack of funds. Accordingly, Sinkhole may recover the reasonable value of the work it performed, less any damage suffered by Pariah's as a result of Sinkhole's breach.

2. Measure of Damages

Since Sinkhole had performed half of a contract with a reasonable value of $100,000, the reasonable value of Sinkhole's partial performance may be assumed to be $50,000. The remaining issue is how much must be deducted from that amount in light of damage caused to Pariah's by Sinkhole's breach. Clearly, Pariah's had to pay a premium over contract price to have the excavation work completed. Had Sinkhole completed the contract, the second half of the work would have cost Pariah's $50,000. Pariah's was forced to pay Gouge'em $75,000, a difference of $25,000. It therefore appears that Sinkhole's recovery must be reduced by $25,000.

3. Duty to Mitigate

Sinkhole might argue that its recovery should not be reduced because the payment of a premium over contract price for the remainder of the excavation work was a failure to mitigate damages. Such an argument would fail. While Pariah's did indeed have a duty to mitigate damages, that duty was satisfied. Gouge'em was the only available substitute contractor, and a timely substitute performance was necessary in order to avoid even greater loss that would have accrued as a result of delay. Accordingly, Sinkhole's recovery must be reduced at least by $25,000 (i.e., from $50,000 to $25,000).

4. Consequential Damages and Foreseeabilty Requirement

The final issue is whether Sinkhole's recovery must be further reduced to reflect the $5,000 loss of the construction trailer. The loss is arguably a result of

Sinkhole's abandonment of the project, but the critical question is whether the foreseeability requirement of *Hadley v. Baxendale* is satisfied. In order to be recoverable, consequential loss must have been foreseeable at the time of contracting, either because such loss results in the "ordinary course of things" from such a breach or because such loss was foreseeable as a result of special circumstances the defendant knew or had reason to know. This can probably be argued either way. Pariah's best chance of reducing Sinkhole's recovery is probably under the second, more particularized prong of the *Hadley* test. Arguably, a professional excavation subcontractor should foresee that abandoning a project midway through performance can create the kind of hazardous condition that caused the loss of the trailer. If so, Sinkhole's recovery is reduced by another $5,000 to $20,000.

Question #3

I. Thick Brick v. Pariah's

1. Modification of Contracts and Good Faith

Yes. The case is a straightforward sale of goods governed by Article 2 of the UCC. 2-209(1) abolishes the pre-existing duty rule for modifications of sales contracts, and the absence of any consideration for the price increase is therefore no impediment to enforcing it. Under Comment 2 to 2-209, such modifications are subject to requirements of good faith, and under 1-103 traditional contract defenses like duress remain available to police modifications. However, the modification at issue does not violate the duty of good faith or meet the elements of duress. It is motivated by a "legitimate commercial reason" within the meaning of Comment 2, since performance at the original price would literally threaten Thick Brick's existence, and there is no evidence of the use of superior bargaining power to gouge Pariah's at a vulnerable moment. Indeed, the August 15 modification did not even leave Thick Brick a profit. The modification is therefore enforceable.

2. Pre-existing Duty Rule

The answer might have been different under the common law. Under the common law pre-existing duty rule, promising to do, or actually doing, what one is already obligated to do is not consideration for a return promise. In this case, the rule would appear to invalidate the modification, as Thick Brick neither promised nor supplied anything new to Pariah's in return for the promise of a price increase. It simply promised to render the contractual performance (delivery of bricks) to which it was already obligated.

3. Unforeseen Circumstances Exception to Pre-existing Duty Rule

The dispositive issue at common law would therefore seem to be whether Thick Brick could establish the elements of the "unforeseen circumstances" exception to the pre-existing duty rule, which has gained widespread acceptance. The exception requires that the modification be reasonable in light of circumstances not foreseeable at the time of contracting. For reasons just mentioned, the modification appears to be a reasonable one. The question is whether the clay shortage creating the need for the modification was unforeseeable at the time of contracting. If it was unforeseeable, the modification is saved by the unforeseen circumstances exception. Otherwise, the modification is invalidated by the pre-existing duty rule. The facts given do not settle the foreseeability question.

Question #4

I. Pariah's v. Thick Brick

1. Cover Remedy and Commercial Reasonableness

Pariah's has sought to avail itself of the cover remedy provided by UCC 2-712. That section permits an aggrieved plaintiff who covers to recover the difference between cover price and contract price, provided the cover transaction is made in good faith, within a commercially reasonable time and on commercially reasonable terms. The cover transaction at issue here was reasonably prompt. However, Thick Brick might argue that the terms of the transaction were unreasonable because the price of bricks had dropped below cover price by the time the date for performance arrived. That argument should fail. Comment 2 to 2-712 specifically preserves the cover remedy even if hindsight reveals that the cover transaction was not the cheapest possible, provided the party effecting cover acted reasonably and in good faith. In this case, Pariah's acted on the basis of advice from experts in the field, and it was their unanimous opinion that the price of bricks would remain at relatively high levels for a long time. Pariah's then covered at the low end of the current market. It thus appears Pariah's acted reasonably, and it should therefore recover cover price ($1.50) less contract price ($1.25, assuming the validity of the August 15 modification), i.e., $0.25 per brick, multiplied by the contract quantity (400,000), for a total of $100,000.

2. Common Law Measure of Damages

The answer would have been different at common law. The common law rule is that an aggrieved buyer is not bound to cover and therefore does so at his own risk. Whether the aggrieved party covers or not, the measure of damages for breach of a forward contract for the sale of goods is the market price on the date fixed for performance less the contract price. Because the market price on the date fixed for performance had dropped to the same level as the original contract price (and below the modified contract price), this damage formula yields a zero recovery for Pariah's.

Question #5

I.   Hot Rivet v. Pariah's

1.   Consideration

The first issue is whether Hot Rivet's agreement to reduce its price was supported by consideration. Pariah's surrender of its "claim" against Hot Rivet for defective performance would not be sufficient consideration. Even under the standards of the more liberal jurisdictions, the surrender of a claim is only consideration for a return promise or performance if the claim has some arguable merit or the party surrendering it holds a good faith belief that it is valid. Here Pariah's claim had no objective merit, and even Pariah's had no belief in its validity. However, Pariah's did agree to pay two weeks early, and, under the peppercorn theory of consideration, even a slight adjustment in the time for payment may be consideration for the substantial price reduction. Accordingly, the compromise agreement does not fail for lack of consideration.

2.   Fraud and Duress

The compromise agreement may, however, be subject to one of two defenses. It may be that it was procured by misrepresentations amounting to fraud, although the exact nature of Pariah's misrepresentations and the degree of Hot Rivet's reliance upon them are not specified. Alternatively, Hot Rivet may have agreed to the price reduction under duress. In order to establish the defense of duress, Hot Rivet would be required to prove that its agreement was procured by Pariah's improper threat, and that the threat left it no reasonable alternative but to agree. Pariah's threat of abusive litigation was certainly improper, but there is insufficient information about Hot Rivet to determine whether it effectively had no choice but to agree.

3.   Novation vs. Accord and Satisfaction

Assuming the compromise agreement is not subject to an affirmative defense, the next question is what type of compromise agreement was made—a substitute contract or an accord and satisfaction. If it was a substitute contract (a "novation"), Pariah's original duty to pay $500,000 was discharged when the agreement was made. If, on the other hand, the agreement was an executory accord, the duty to pay $500,000 would only be discharged by actual payment of the compromise amount (i.e., by actual satisfaction). The distinction is significant in this case because the compromise agreement was breached by Pariah's failure to pay anything whatsoever, and because the consequence of the breach varies depending on the type of compromise. If the compromise agreement was a substitute contract, the original duty of payment was already discharged and Hot Rivet may only sue for the compromise amount, $250,000. If, on the other hand, the agreement was an attempt at accord and satisfaction, the original duty of payment was not discharged, and Hot Rivet may sue either on the original duty or the accord. Obviously, Hot Rivet would sue on the original duty to pay $500,000. Given that Hot Rivet's original right to payment was liquidated, contingent only upon the passage of a short period of time, and not subject to any bona fide dispute, it would be unreasonable to assume Hot Rivet intended to discharge it immediately in return for Pariah's mere promise to pay, rather than actual payment. Accordingly, it is more reasonable to regard the compromise agreement as a failed accord and satisfaction, and Hot Rivet may therefore sue Pariah's for breach of the original duty to pay $500,000. Hot Rivet should recover that amount.

CONTRACTS
MULTIPLE CHOICE

100
QUESTIONS

ANSWER SHEET

Print or copy this answer sheet to answer all multiple choice questions.

1. A B C D	26. A B C D	51. A B C D	76. A B C D
2. A B C D	27. A B C D	52. A B C D	77. A B C D
3. A B C D	28. A B C D	53. A B C D	78. A B C D
4. A B C D	29. A B C D	54. A B C D	79. A B C D
5. A B C D	30. A B C D	55. A B C D	80. A B C D
6. A B C D	31. A B C D	56. A B C D	81. A B C D
7. A B C D	32. A B C D	57. A B C D	82. A B C D
8. A B C D	33. A B C D	58. A B C D	83. A B C D
9. A B C D	34. A B C D	59. A B C D	84. A B C D
10. A B C D	35. A B C D	60. A B C D	85. A B C D
11. A B C D	36. A B C D	61. A B C D	86. A B C D
12. A B C D	37. A B C D	62. A B C D	87. A B C D
13. A B C D	38. A B C D	63. A B C D	88. A B C D
14. A B C D	39. A B C D	64. A B C D	89. A B C D
15. A B C D	40. A B C D	65. A B C D	90. A B C D
16. A B C D	41. A B C D	66. A B C D	91. A B C D
17. A B C D	42. A B C D	67. A B C D	92. A B C D
18. A B C D	43. A B C D	68. A B C D	93. A B C D
19. A B C D	44. A B C D	69. A B C D	94. A B C D
20. A B C D	45. A B C D	70. A B C D	95. A B C D
21. A B C D	46. A B C D	71. A B C D	96. A B C D
22. A B C D	47. A B C D	72. A B C D	97. A B C D
23. A B C D	48. A B C D	73. A B C D	98. A B C D
24. A B C D	49. A B C D	74. A B C D	99. A B C D
25. A B C D	50. A B C D	75. A B C D	100. A B C D

CONTRACTS QUESTIONS

1. Patricia's employer fired her after only three months in the job, in breach of a twelve-month employment contract. Patricia is entitled to recover as damages

    A. her salary for twelve months.

    B. her salary for nine months.

    C. her salary for nine months, less what she could have earned in another job had she made reasonable efforts to find another suitable job.

    D. nothing, because employment contracts must provide for liquidated damages.

2. Paul is a law student and needs some extra cash. He puts up posters saying that he wants to sell his skis. Dorothy agrees to buy them for $200. She never comes up with the money, though, and she breaches their contract.

    A. Paul has a duty to try to resell the skis.

    B. If Paul does not try to resell the skis, he will nevertheless be treated as if he had.

    C. Dorothy has a duty to find another buyer for the skis.

    D. All of the above.

3. Under the same facts as the preceding question, how much is Paul most likely to recover, assuming the contract price is essentially the same as the fair

market value and that it is not too hard to sell skis this time of year?

A. $200.

B. $200, with a possibility of large punitive damages for willful breach.

C. Paul will probably be limited to specific performance.

D. Probably close to nothing.

Questions 4-7 refer to these facts:

Paula knits baby blankets in her spare time, selling as many as she can. She has never had trouble knitting enough to meet the needs of the buyers; she has more trouble finding buyers than knitting blankets. Darlene and Paula agree orally that Paula will knit a blanket for Darlene's new baby for $150, with the blanket to be delivered about a month later. Darlene is to pay at that time. The blanket is to have the baby's name and birthdate knitted in large pink figures in the middle of the blanket. Two days later, however, Darlene calls Paula and refuses to go ahead with the deal. Paula has already bought the yarn—the only necessary material for the blanket—for $20, and the yarn cannot be returned to the store.

4. Paula

A. has no contract with Darlene because of the statute of frauds.

B. has a contract with Darlene, but the contract is unenforceable under the statute of frauds because there is no writing.

C. has a contract with Darlene, and the contract is enforceable despite the absence of a writing because of the "part performance" exception to the statute of frauds.

D. has an enforceable contract with Darlene.

5. Assuming that Paula and Darlene have an enforceable contract, Paula's damages as measured by the restitution interest are

   A. zero.

   B. $20.

   C. $130.

   D. $150.

6. Assuming that Paula and Darlene have an enforceable contract, Paula's damages as measured by the reliance interest are

   A. zero.

   B. $20.

   C. $130.

   D. $150.

7. Suppose that Darlene did not inform Paula of the breach till after Paula finished knitting the blanket. Assuming that Paula and Darlene have an enforceable contract, Paula is entitled to recover

    A.   zero, or close to zero.

    B. $20.

    C. $130.

    D. $150.

8.   Upon defendant's breach of a contract for the sale of goods, plaintiff is entitled to specific performance

    A.   if plaintiff cannot reasonably obtain cover.

    B.   only if the goods are unique, such as works of art.

    C.   as a matter of course.

    D.   only if defendant does not have "clean hands."

9.   Specific performance is most likely to be available in which of the following cases?

    A.   For the sale of land.

    B.   For construction of a large shopping mall.

    C.   For the painting of a portrait.

    D.   For the sale of goods.

10.   A court is most likely to stretch to interpret

    A.   an agreement that the parties intended to be binding.

B.   an offer.

C.   an acceptance.

D.   a counteroffer.

Read the following provisions from the UCC. Then answer question 11 - 14.

"Termination" occurs when either party pursuant to a power created by agreement or law puts an end to the contract otherwise than for its breach. On "termination" all obligations which are still executory on both sides are discharged but any right based on prior breach or performance survives.

"Cancellation" occurs when either party puts an end to the contract for breach by the other and its effect is the same as that of "termination" except that the cancelling party also retains any remedy for breach of the whole contract or any unperformed balance.

11.   Alberta and Bob make a contract. Bob breaches, so Alberta puts an end to the contract. Alberta's action will constitute a

A.   termination.

B.   cancellation.

C.   both of the above.

D.   none of the above.

12. By her action, Alberta

    A. must give up any remedy for breach.

    B. must discharge Bob's liabilities.

    C. retains her right to sue Bob for damages.

    D. none of the above.

13. Stephens Co. and Boyd's Inc. contract in writing for Boyd's to buy from Stephens 100 cases of sterile gauze pads a month for twelve months. The contract states, among other things, "Either party may end this Agreement by giving written notice to the other party at least ten calendar days before the date on which the notice is to take effect." On June 16, Boyd's hand delivers a written notice to Stephens, saying only this: "We are putting an end to our contract pursuant to the provision therein. This notice is to take effect as soon as possible under the applicable clause of the contract."

    A. The contract will be terminated before the end of June.

    B. The contract will be cancelled before the end of June.

    C. The contract is terminated immediately when Stephens receives the notice.

    D. The contract is cancelled immediately when Stephens receives the notice.

14. In July, Boyd's discovers that the pads in the last shipment before the notice were not sterile, leading

to a potentially large claim by Boyd's against Stephens.

    A.   Boyd's has waived its claim by ending the contract.

    B.   Boyd's claim is preserved under the statutory provision on termination.

    C.   Boyd's claim is preserved under the statutory provision on cancellation.

    D.   Stephens will likely prevail on the defense that it has been discharged.

15.   Seller publishes a catalog listing prices for various office supplies. Buyer mails an order for 100 boxes of paper clips at the catalog price. Seller ships the clips upon receiving the order. Ten days later, Seller sends an invoice to the Buyer, billing the Buyer according to the terms in the catalog.

    A.   The catalog constitutes an offer.

    B.   Buyer's order was an offer.

    C.   Seller's shipment was an offer.

    D.   Seller's shipment was a rejection and counteroffer.

16.   Using the same facts as the preceding question:

    A.   Buyer and Seller did not form a contract.

    B.   Buyer and Seller formed a bilateral contract.

  C. Buyer and Seller formed a unilateral contract.

  D. There is a contract between Buyer and Seller only to the extent specified in UCC § 2-207 (governing the "battle of the forms").

17. Contractual rights generally

  A. may be assigned.

  B. may be delegated.

  C. may be assigned only to a creditor or donee.

  D. may not be assigned or delegated.

18. Contractual duties

  A. may be delegated only in personal services contracts.

  B. may be delegated or assigned only if the duty is fully extinguished in the delegating or assigning party.

  C. if delegated, still remain in the delegating party, who is then much like a surety or guarantor.

  D. are *per se* not subject to delegation or assignment.

19. Under contract law, consequential damages

A. Cannot be disclaimed entirely but may be set at a certain amount.

B. Can often be disclaimed entirely, since a complete disclaimer of consequential damages is not necessarily unconscionable.

C. Are not recoverable in a contract action unless there is also a tort.

D. Cannot be awarded in arbitration.

20. Plaintiff agreed to work for Defendant for 12 months for $3000 a quarter, payable quarterly. After nine months, Plaintiff quits, which he concedes is a material breach of the contract. He has been paid for the first six months work, but not the last three. He sues. If he recovers anything, he is most likely to be compensated according to which measure of damages?

A. Expectancy.

B. Reliance.

C. Restitution.

D. Incidental.

21. A job application for a large fast-food chain contains the following clause: "Applicant understands that this application confers no legal rights. Applicant agrees to arbitrate any disputes with employer." The applicant signs the application. He is not hired, which he thinks is wrong. He wants to sue. What is the best

argument that the arbitration clause is not binding?

A.   The clause is not binding for lack of consideration.

B.   The clause is not binding because it violates the policy against arbitration.

C.   The clause is not binding because of the parol evidence rule.

D.   The clause is not binding because of the statute of frauds.

22.   Betty has a piece of paper saying the following. "I offer to sell Betty Buyer the farm known as 'Stone Bluff' for $300,000. This offer to remain open for five days from today. [Signed] Sam Seller, May 17, 2003." Betty has not done anything yet.

A.   The offer cannot be revoked until May 21, 2003.

B.   The offer cannot be revoked until May 22, 2003.

C.   The offer can be revoked at any time.

D.   The offer cannot be revoked because it qualifies as a "firm offer" under the UCC.

23. A physician says to his patient, Gwen, "I guarantee you a 100% good hand after surgery." Gwen had suffered from a bad hand for years because of an injury. The physician had talked to Gwen over the course of several months, suggesting the surgery to her because it involved a kind of surgery of particular interest to the physician. Through his negligence, the physician makes the hand even worse after surgery that it was before. He is liable

   A. In tort.

   B. On an express contract.

   C. On an implied contract.

   D. All of the above.

24. Consider a different case now. A patient, John, goes to see a doctor for the first time. The receptionist makes a copy of John's insurance card and has him fill out forms having to do with his medical history. If John later incurs damages because of the doctor's care and sues the physician, which is the most likely cause of action?

   A. Promissory estoppel

   B. Express contract

   C. Implied contract

   D. Quasi-contract

Question 25 - 18 are based on these facts:

Carl has a construction business. Last week he visited Hugh to give a quote for a one-room addition to

Hugh's house. Hugh wants the addition completed for $10,000 by the end of August. Hugh said that he would provide the materials and asked Carl to provide the labor. Carl said, "Sure, I can do it for $10,000."

Hugh replied, "Great. When can you start?"

"Mid-July."

"And you'll still finish by the end of August? My daughter's getting married then, and we'll need the room."

"Oh, yeah. No problem," Carl said.

"Okay," Hugh said.

"Okay," Carl said.

No money—or anything else—has changed hands.

25.   Carl has been offered a large and lucrative job that will require all summer and that would preclude him from doing Hugh's job during that time. He asks you whether he can take that job.

    A.   Yes, because there is no consideration yet for his arrangement with Hugh.

    B.   Yes, because Carl and Hugh have not even reached the stage of offer and acceptance.

    C.   Yes. Although Carl and Hugh have entered into a contract, its enforcement is barred by the statute of frauds.

    D.   No, because Carl is already bound by a contract to Hugh.

26. Assume that Carl decides that his honor if nothing else requires him to forego the big job. Carl begins work for Hugh on July 15, but after watching the building for a week, Hugh remains nervous about having the room done in time. He tells Carl his concern. Carl says, "Hey, don't worry about it. I'll tell you what: I'll give you 100 bucks a day for every day I go past the deadline." Hugh gratefully accepts, and they shake hands.

    A. The $100/day clause is invalid because it violates the pre-existing duty rule.

    B. The $100/day clause is unenforceable because it is not in writing.

    C. The $100/day clause is valid because the pre-existing duty rule has been abolished.

    D. The $100/day clause is valid as a side agreement.

27. Assume that the conversation about the $100/day never took place. If Carl takes on Hugh's job but does not finish in time, he

    A. Will not be liable for damages.

    B. Will be liable only for liquidated damages.

    C. Will be liable for damages according to a formula set by the UCC.

    D. None of the above.

28. Assume that the conversation about the $100/day never took place and that Carl takes on Hugh's job but does not finish in time. If Hugh therefore has

to pay $300 per day in hotel costs for wedding guests that would have stayed at his house but for the unfinished construction, Carl will likely avoid liability for those damages:

A.   Because he never said he would take on that liability.

B.   Because of the *Hadley v. Baxendale* rule.

C.   Because the harm is too unusual or remote.

D.   None of the above arguments is likely to prevail.

29.   Liquidated damages clauses

A.   Are not valid.

B.   Are now valid because of economic arguments associated with Judge Richard Posner.

C.   Are sometimes valid, depending on the circumstances.

D.   Are valid at common law but not under the UCC.

30. Chester E. Overton, a highly compensated executive, makes the following contracts: (1) Chester is to have his portrait painted by Ansel Artiste, one of the busiest portrait painters in the world, who turns away almost everyone because he is so busy. Ansel only agreed to paint Chester because Chester is so famous. (2) Chester agrees to buy a new Ford Thunderbird convertible, which reminds him of his youth. (3) He agrees to buy his friend's yacht. You may assume that all of the contracts are valid and enforceable. Before any of the contracts is performed, a corporate scandal comes to light, and Chester loses his job and his money. He breaches all of the contracts. Which plaintiff is most likely to have a claim for the lost profit?

    A.   The portrait painter

    B.   The car dealer

    C.   The friend

    D.   None of the above.

31. Joy and Todd reach an oral agreement about each of the following. Which of them is enforceable?

    A.   The sale of a new car.

    B.   A lease of an apartment for one year.

    C.   A six-month loan of $1000.

    D.   None of the above.

32. Intended beneficiaries generally fall into which categories?

    A.   Donee and creditor.

    B.   Employers and insurance companies.

    C.   Lessors and lessees.

    D.   Intended beneficiaries cannot be generalized into categories.

33.   Which of the following will ordinarily support a legally binding contract?

    A.   Past consideration.

    B.   Moral consideration.

    C.   Nominal consideration.

    D.   None of the above.

34.   The implied warranty of merchantability under the UCC

    A.   Can be disclaimed only in writing.

    B.   Can be disclaimed by the use of "as is" or the like.

    C.   Attaches to all sales of goods unless it is disclaimed.

    D.   All of the above.

35.   The UCC fitness warranty

    A.   Can be disclaimed in writing, although the disclaimer must be conspicuous.

B.   Cannot be disclaimed by the use of "as is" or the like.

C.   Assures a buyer that goods will fit their ordinary purpose.

D.   All of the above.

36.   Under the statute of frauds contained in UCC § 2-201, which of the following may be omitted from the writing?

A.   Quantity.

B.   Price.

C.   Signature.

D.   None of the above.

Question 37 - 44 are based on these facts:

By letter dated February 1, a farmer offers to deliver to buyer 100 tons of grain on April 15, for a price of $250 per ton, payment to be made two weeks before delivery. Buyer accepts by letter dated February 5.

37.   On March 1, Seller sends Buyer a fax saying, "Due to labor action by agricultural workers, we may not be able to deliver until April 22." Buyer would be best advised to

A.   Send a letter to Seller stating that Seller is in breach and Buyer will not pay until after delivery.

B.   Telephone the Seller as soon as possible to notify Seller of possible damages.

C.   Send Seller a letter asking for an assurance that Seller will perform by the contract date.

D.   Wait and see what happens on the delivery date.

38.   Assume that Seller does in fact tender delivery one week late.

A.   Seller will not be liable to buyer if the one-week delay is not a substantial impairment in the value of the contract.

B.   Seller will not be liable to buyer if the one-week delay is not a material breach.

C.   Seller may be liable for damages but the contract will remain in place, unless the delay is a material breach or results in substantial impairment.

D.   Regardless of whether the delay substantially impairs the value of the contract, Buyer may tell the Seller that Buyer does not want the goods and that the contract is off.

39.   Which of the following changes would result in a change in your answers to the preceding two questions?

A.   The contract called for delivery of half the grain on April 1 and the other half on April 15.

B. The contract disclaimed liability for consequential damages.

C. Either "A" or "B" would change the answers.

D. Neither "A" nor "B" would change the answers.

40. Using only the original facts, as stated before the first question in this set, assume that Seller fails to deliver any grain at all on April 15.

A. Buyer may obtain replacement goods if doing so is commercially reasonable.

B. Buyer need not obtain replacement goods and may simply sue for damages.

C. Buyer may do either "A" or "B," but "A" is probably better advised.

D. Buyer may do either "A" or "B," but "B" is probably better advised.

41. Using the same facts as stated in the previous question, assume that Buyer on April 16 calls a well-respected commodities broker. The broker obtains replacement grain for Buyer on April 17 for $275 per ton plus the customary brokerage commission. The market price on April 15 was $270 per ton and that the market price on April 16 and 17 was $275 per ton. You may assume that Buyer was excused from prepaying and did not prepay.

A. Buyer will likely recover $2500 plus the brokerage commission in damages.

B.   Buyer will likely recover $2500 in damages.

C.   Buyer will likely recover $2000 plus the brokerage commission in damages.

D.   Buyer will likely recover $2100 in damages.

42.   Use the same facts as stated in the previous question, except assume that Buyer immediately files suit instead of trying to get replacement grain.

A.   Buyer will likely recover $2625 in damages.

B.   Buyer will likely recover $2500 in damages.

C.   Buyer will likely recover $2000 in damages.

D.   Buyer will likely recover $2100 plus the brokerage commission in damages.

43.   Using only the original facts, as stated before the first question in this set, assume that Buyer refuses to take or pay for the grain because the price of grain on April 15 is $200 per ton.

A.   Seller will likely recover $25,000.

B.   Seller will likely recover $20,000.

C.   Seller will likely recover $5000.

D.   Seller will likely recover $50,000.

44.   The contract at issue in the preceding questions is best characterized as a

A. Unilateral contract.

B. Bilateral contract.

C. Output contract.

D. Requirements contract.

45. If a court finds that a writing is partially integrated, a party could introduce evidence before the jury of

A. orally agreed terms consistent with but additional to those in the writing.

B. later oral agreements.

C. fraud.

D. all of the above.

46. Hugh, a college student, says to Ida, a secretary, "I will sell you my car for $2000." Ida says, "Okay, that sounds good. I'll take it."

A. Article 2 of the UCC governs this transaction.

B. Article 2 of the UCC will serve only as persuasive authority in this transaction.

C. Article 2 has no authority in this transaction, except to fill gaps left by the Restatement.

D. Article 2 will imply a warranty of merchantability in this transaction.

47. In the preceding question,

    A. Hugh and Ida have a contract.

    B. If Ida sues to enforce the contract, she would lose if Hugh asserts the Statute of Frauds.

    C. Hugh and Ida do not have a contract because of the Statute of Frauds.

    D. A and B but not C.

48. Best Bearings Inc. is in the business of selling ball bearings. It needed some new furniture for its executive offices, and its president went to Standard Supply Co., where she looked around and noted what pieces she liked. After thinking about which items to choose, she had the purchasing department send a purchase order for specific model numbers. A week later, Standard Supply Co. delivered the specified furniture, except for one piece: because Standard was out of teak credenzas, it sent a cherry one instead. Standard sent an invoice a week after delivering the furniture, stating the appropriate (lower) price for the cherry credenza. You may assume for this and the following questions that the forms do not say anything relevant aside from what you have been told.

    A. There is no contract between the parties because the forms of the parties do not match.

    B. There is no contract between the parties because the mirror image rule is violated.

C.   There is no contract between the parties unless Best agrees to accept the cherry credenza.

D.   There is a contract between the parties.

49.   Using the same facts,

A.   Best Bearings is a merchant.

B.   Best Bearings is not a merchant with respect to goods of the kind.

C.   Best Bearings is not a merchant.

D.   A and B but not C.

50.   Lydia and Tony sign a one-year lease. Tony moves in without a hitch, pays the stipulated $400-a-month rent for four months, and lives there happily. The lease is in writing. Then Lydia learns that her rent is well below market, which would be about $500 a month. She explains the situation to Tony, and he agrees to pay $450 a month for the remainder of the lease. They shake on the deal. A few days later, Tony changes his mind.

A.   Tony is obligated to pay $450 a month because the parties have modified the contract in good faith.

B.   Tony is obligated to pay $450 a month because Lydia had an objectively demonstrable reason for the change in rent.

C.   Tony is obligated to pay $450 a month because consideration was inadequate.

D.   Tony is only obligated to pay $400 a month.

51.   Saul invested in the real estate market, which did very well. He no longer needed to provide for himself and his wife, but he wanted to provide for his daughter Darlene, who had a family of her own. Saul sold a large property to Betty, who agreed to pay for it by paying $3000 a month for thirty years. They drew up the contract so that Betty would make the payments to Darlene, and Saul and Betty both signed. Darlene did not. Everything went fine for a while, but now the payments have ceased, and Saul (who lives in a distant and sunny spot now) doesn't want to be bothered. He tells Darlene to take care of it. Can she?

A.   Darlene can sue Betty as a creditor beneficiary.

B.   Darlene can sue Betty as a donee beneficiary.

C.   Darlene cannot sue Betty because Darlene is an intended beneficiary.

D.   Darlene cannot sue Betty because Darlene is not a party to the contract.

52.   Using the same facts, consider an alternative theory for Darlene. Should she succeed in any of the following claims?

A.   Darlene can sue Betty on a delegation theory because Saul delegated the duty to Darlene.

B.   Darlene can sue Betty on a delegation theory because Darlene is Saul's delegate.

C.   Darlene can sue Betty on an assignment theory because Saul assigned Betty to pay Darlene.

D.   None of the above.

53.   Using the same facts, suppose that Darlene informed Betty that Darlene no longer wanted to receive payment herself but was assigning her rights to her own grown son (Saul's grandson) Gary. Betty made payments to Gary for a while, but then Gary and Darlene fell out. Darlene now informs Betty to start paying Darlene herself again, but Gary says to continue paying him.

A.   Because of the assignment, Darlene has lost the right to be paid.

B.   Darlene still has the right to be paid because the assignment created rights in Gary without prejudice to her own.

C.   Betty must pay Darlene because Gary was merely Darlene's delegate, and she has revoked the delegation.

D.   None of the above.

54.   Suppose Saul told Darlene that he would give her $10,000 a year for the rest of his life because of his love and affection for her. Darlene thanked her father and soon quit her job as a CPA (which she hated) and became a schoolteacher (which she loves, but which pays less). Saul and Darlene have now fallen out, and Saul refuses to pay anymore. Under the bargain theory of consideration, Saul's promise to pay Darlene $10,000 a year

A.   is supported by consideration because it induced her reliance.

B.   is supported by adequate moral consideration.

C.   is not supported by consideration but is nevertheless enforceable under the moral obligation exception for promises "in consideration of love and affection."

D.   is not supported by consideration.

55.   Using the same facts, Darlene's best cause of action against Saul is

A.   rescission.

B.   breach of contract.

C.   promissory estoppel.

D.   quasi-contract.

56.   If Betty were to succeed in a cause of action against Saul,

A.   a court should award expectancy damages, but many have limited recovery to restitution.

B.   a court should award reliance damages, but many have allowed expectancy.

C.   specific performance is most likely because this is a family promise.

D. a court will probably enter an injunction against Saul.

57. Suppose Saul signed a writing stating, "I promise to give Alma Mater School of Law one million dollars ($1 million) on or before January 15, 2002." He signed his name at the bottom. His promise, in virtually all jurisdictions today,

A. is binding as long as the word "SEAL" appears near his signature.

B. is binding as long as the word "SEAL" appears near his signature and is circled.

C. is binding as long as the word "SEAL" appears near his signature and is circled in whole or in part, or the letters "L.S." appear at the end of the signature line.

D. is binding, if at all, for reasons not having to do with a seal.

58. Tina Finnegan has operated a plumbing sales and service business for twenty years. She signed a contract with one of her suppliers stipulating that if the goods sold were defective, damages would be limited to replacement of the defective items. One of these items was defective, and when installed, caused $750 in property damage to one of Tina's biggest customers, which is a steel mill. The limitation of remedy, which is now being invoked by the supplier, was one of fifteen paragraphs, written in plain English, on the reverse of a form contract. Above the signature line on the front of the contract was the statement, "THIS CONTRACT IS SUBJECT

TO THE TERMS AND CONDITIONS ON THE REVERSE HEREOF." The limitation of remedy is

A. unconscionable because any limitation of consequential damages is unconscionable.

B. likely unconscionable because a limitation for property damage is prima facie unconscionable.

C. likely invalid because it was in a form contract.

D. unlikely to be found unconscionable.

59. Terms

A. in contracts of adhesion are generally invalid.

B. that are sent after a consumer has placed an order are generally invalid.

C. that are sent after a consumer has placed an order are valid according to several prominent cases if the consumer can return the product for a refund.

D. A and B

60. Under the doctrine of mutual or unilateral mistake, which of the following is a "mistake"?

A. A belief that a cow is barren when in fact she is with calf.

B. A belief that the price of a good sold will rise in the future.

C.   A belief that the price of the contracted-for service will rise in the future.

D.   An assumption that an earthquake will not strike.

61.   Which of the following requires an unusually high standard of proof (i.e., more than the usual "preponderance of the evidence" standard)?

A.   Reformation

B.   Mutual mistake

C.   Unilateral mistake

D.   Fraud

62.   Consider the following contracts. Who is most likely to invoke a defense of frustration of purpose?

A.   A buyer

B.   A seller

C.   A lessor

D.   A licensor of real property

63.   Which of the following is most likely to be held void (as opposed to voidable)? An apparent agreement vitiated by

A.   infancy

B. incapacity

C. duress by force

D. A and C

64. In an agreement signed on February 8, VSU hired
    Bob Bowdell to be head football coach starting on
    March 1 and continuing through February 28 of the
    following year, at an annual salary of $500,000.
    On February 15, the president of VSU learned that
    another, much more successful, football coach was
    available. VSU struck a deal with him on February
    18, and that same day informed Bowdell that his
    services would not be needed. Today is February
    19.

    A. VSU has breached the contract.

    B. VSU's action constitutes anticipatory
        repudiation.

    C. VSU will not have breached the contract until
        March 1, or perhaps March 2.

    D. A and B

65. Owen and Willa make a contract in which Willa is
    to work for two weeks, and Owen is to pay her at
    the end of the second week.

    A. Payment and doing the work are concurrent
        conditions.

    B. Payment is a condition precedent.

    C. Payment is a condition subsequent.

D.   Doing the work is a condition precedent.

66.   Stella and Beth make a contract for the sale of corn. Stella is to deliver the corn in two weeks and is to collect the payment on delivery.

A.   payment and delivery are concurrent conditions.

B.   payment is a condition precedent.

C.   payment is a condition subsequent.

D.   delivery is a condition precedent.

67.   A construction contract includes the following clause: "Any work furnished by the Contractor, the material or workmanship of which is defective or which is not fully in accord with the specifications, in every respect, will be rejected and is to be immediately torn down and replaced, whenever discovered." The contractor has substantially performed the contract, but has inadvertently breached certain parts of the contract and permanently installed some fixtures of the wrong brand. A significant part of the structure will indeed have to be "torn down and replaced" if the fixtures are to be changed. This clause is likely to be held

A.   a constructive condition.

B.   an express condition.

C.   a condition subsequent.

D.   a promise.

68.   If the preceding provision is not satisfied (i.e., the contractor does not replace the fixtures), the owner

A.   will still have to pay the contractor.

B.   will have a remedy for damages (if there are any).

C.   will not have to pay the contractor.

D.   A and B

69.   In the preceding problem, the contractor will most likely be liable for

A.   expectancy damages.

B.   the cost to do the work as the contract requires.

C.   the difference (if any) between the value of the building as it is and the value of the building as it should have been built.

D.   A and C.

70.   Your client has ordered 104,000 pounds of inedible beef udders (used for making pet food) for $19,000 in a signed contract, delivery on May 5. On May 5, only 98,000 pounds show up. Your client calls and asks if she is required to accept the short delivery. Your advice:

A. No, because the delivery does not satisfy the perfect tender rule.

B. No, because such a variation (three tons!) would substantially impair the value of the contract to her.

C. Possibly, because the perfect tender rule has been abolished

D. It depends. You need to ask your client whether any usage of trade, course of dealing, or course of performance would permit such a variation in delivery quantity.

71. You may now assume that the signed agreement of the parties calls for delivery of 104,000 pounds of inedible beef udders with an allowed variation in delivery of no more than 1000 pounds (with a price adjustment depending on the variation). On the date stipulated for delivery, 98,000 pounds show up. Your client calls and asks, "Do I have to accept the short delivery?" Your advice:

A. No, because the delivery does not satisfy the perfect tender rule.

B. It depends on whether this variation substantially impairs the value of the contract to her.

C. It depends on whether this variation substantially impairs the value of the contract to a reasonable person in the circumstances.

D. Yes, because this variation will not satisfy the factors for material breach.

72.   Now suppose in the preceding problem that after asking whether she has to accept the delivery, your client continues, "The reason I'm wondering is that I can now get inedible beef udders even cheaper from another supplier, and I'd really rather save the money." You say,

    A.   The reason doesn't really matter. It all just depends on whether this is a substantial impairment in the value of the contract to her.

    B.   The reason doesn't really matter. It all just depends on whether this is a substantial impairment in the value of the contract to a reasonable person in the circumstances.

    C.   The seller might not let her get away with this. As long as the seller reasonably thought this shipment would be okay, the seller has the right to cure the short delivery.

    D.   As there is no material breach, she has to accept anyway.

73.   In the preceding problem, if you were representing the seller, which of the following is the most promising basis for argument?

    A.   The Article 1 requirement that all parties act reasonably, as your client tells you this rejection would be considered unreasonable

    B.   Good faith, as your client tells you that rejection because of a price change is viewed in the industry as being unfair

C. Usage of trade, since your client tells you that industry custom allows variations of 10%

D. The Article 2 gap filler for quantity, which refers to a reasonableness standard

74. Barbara Wonell is taking Corporations next year, and she and Joe Tuel, an upperclassman, agree that he will sell her his used book for $25. They agree that payment and delivery will take place next week.

A. They have an enforceable contract.

B. They do not yet have a contract because no consideration has passed yet.

C. They do not yet have a contract because there is no reliance.

D. The contract is not enforceable because it is not in writing.

75. After making his agreement with Wonell, Tuel saw one of his friends, Tom, who also is planning to take Corporations. Tom agreed to pay $30 for the Corporations book, and Tuel agreed. Wonell found out about this from a reliable source before she had paid for the book and before Tuel had delivered it to anyone.

A. Tuel's offer to Wonell is revoked.

B. Tuel has a contract with Tom, but not with Wonell.

C.   Tuel's offer to Tom was invalid for formation of a contract.

D.   Tuel is bound by enforceable contracts with both Wonell and Tom.

76.   Claire, a graduate student, agrees to sell her old TV to her friend John, a computer programmer, for $400. This transaction will be governed

A.   by Article 1 of the UCC.

B.   by Article 2 of the UCC.

C.   by the common law and not the UCC, because the buyer and seller are not merchants.

D.   A and B

77.   A few days after they made their initial agreement, they realize that neither one of them has a car, and Claire and John subsequently agree that Claire will deliver the TV to John's apartment without any further charge, even though that means she will have to pay for a cab. (They live within walking distance of each other under ordinary conditions, but it is too far to carry a TV.) You should recall that the default rule calls for delivery at the seller's place.

A.   Under their initial agreement, John was required to pick up the TV.

B.   The default rule did not apply to the initial agreement because Claire is not a merchant.

C.   The default rule did not apply to the initial agreement because Claire is not a merchant with respect to goods of the kind.

D.   The lack of delivery term in the initial agreement would have made the contract too uncertain to enforce, had they not cured the deficiency in their subsequent agreement.

78.   Claire and John's subsequent agreement is

A.   not binding because of the pre-existing duty rule.

B.   binding.

C.   binding only if John relies on it.

D.   binding only if John relies on it to his detriment.

79.   Blissfully unaware of these legal questions, Claire takes a cab to John's place, planning to walk home after dropping off the TV. The cab fare was $10. When John answers the door, he says he no longer wants the TV, and he refuses to take or pay for it. As she's standing on the street with the TV, another friend of Claire's (Tim) walks by. Upon finding out what has happened, Tim says, "What a coincidence! I need another TV, and I'll pay you $400 for that one and take it off your hands." Claire happily agrees and hands over the TV. As against John, Claire's damages as measured by the restitution interest are

A.   zero.

B. $10.

C. $400.

D. $410.

80.   If Claire were actually to file suit against John, the likely damage award would be

A.   zero or nominal damages.

B. $400.

C. $410.

D.   at least $400, plus reasonably likely punitive damages.

81.   In its OCP Plant, an oil refinery uses a machine called a masticator to chew up rubber, which is then added to boiling oil to make certain kinds of motor oil. The masticator breaks down and needs to be sent for repair. The refinery contracts with a railroad to deliver the masticator to the manufacturer by June 1. The railroad does not deliver it until June 15, causing the OCP Plant to be closed for an additional two weeks. The refinery can probably recover

A.   its lost net profit for two weeks.

B.   its lost gross profit for two weeks.

C.   what it would cost to rent a similar masticator for two weeks.

D.   nothing.

82.   Assume now that the refinery sues for lost profits
       for two weeks. The strongest argument for the
       defendant on that issue is that

    A.   profits are generally speculative.

    B.   profits are too uncertain to be recovered.

    C.   shutdown of the plant was not foreseeable.

    D.   a two-week delay is not a force majeure.

83.   Your client has spent $400,000 in preparing to
       perform a big new contract. The other party to the
       contract, has just sent a fax saying, "In no
       circumstances will we perform." You would be
       most likely to sue for reliance damages if your client

    A.   had a great bargain under the contract.

    B.   it is not clear whether your client would have
          made a profit under the contract.

    C.   the defendant is especially well financed and
          has a lot of money for litigation.

    D.   your client is especially well financed and has
          a lot of money for litigation.

84.   Assume that you do actually sue for reliance
       damages for the reason given in the preceding
       problem. You would expect

A.   not to recover reliance damages, because expectancy and specific performance are the only remedies available in contract.

B.   not to recover reliance damages because expectancy is the cap on damages.

C.   to recover reliance damages, which are the plaintiff's right.

D.   to recover reliance damages because defendant probably could not make the necessary showing to reduce damages.

85.   Buyer and Seller, previously unknown to each other, make a contract for the sale of cotton to arrive on a ship named HELENA. Unknown to Buyer and Seller, several ships are named HELENA. Buyer intends the HELENA scheduled to arrive in October; Seller intends the HELENA scheduled to arrive in December. Absent other facts,

A.   the contract is for cotton on the first ship.

B.   the contract is for cotton on the latest ship.

C.   the contract will be specifically enforced.

D.   there is no contract.

86.   Lynn was living in Indiana when she got a call from Weigel & Weigel, a firm in Chicago. Weigel said that if Lynn would quit her job and actually go to Chicago and start work right away, she would get the open associate position in the firm. She said she would think about it. She slept on it that night. When she woke up, she knew it was the right thing to do. She called her current employer

and quit her job, then got in her car and drove to Chicago. She started her first project that afternoon. Assume that an employment contract is made in the state where the last necessary act was done to form the employment contract. You may also assume the relevant court follows the Restatement (Second) of Contracts. The employment contract was made

A.   in Indiana because performance began there.

B.   in Indiana because a beginning of performance was tendered there.

C.   in Indiana because performance was there.

D.   in Illinois.

87.   In the preceding situation, Weigel

A.   could have revoked the offer at any time before Lynn started work.

B.   could have revoked the offer at any time before Lynn got to Chicago.

C.   could not revoke the offer after the initial telephone call.

could not revoke the offer after Lynn started on her way to Chicago.

88.   The answer in the preceding question results from

A.   the formation of the employment contract.

B.   the revocability of offers until they are accepted.

C.   an option contract.

D.   bilateral contract formation.

89.   After a trade show, Bob and Sarah are having a drink in the hotel bar. Sarah is an agent for a manufacturer of hot-rolled steel. Bob is an agent for a tool-and-die company. You may assume they have the authority to bind their companies. They discuss a sale of hot-rolled steel for $275 per metric ton. "Really?" Bob asks. "That's a great price."

Sarah responds, "Definitely. Do we have a deal?"

"Absolutely," Bob says. They shake hands.

A.   The parties have a contract.

B.   The parties have a contract subject to the parol evidence rule.

C.   The parties would have a contract but for the statute of frauds.

D.   The parties would have a contract but for the lack of certainty.

90.   In the preceding question, suppose that at the end of the conversation, Bob had said, "Absolutely, I can guarantee you that we'll buy all our hot-rolled steel from you for the next three months. That will be at least 300 metric tons a month." Sarah responded, "Fantastic, it's a deal."

A.   The parties have a requirements contract.

B.   The parties have an output contract.

C.   The parties would have a contract but for the statute of frauds.

D.   The parties would have a contract but for the lack of certainty.

91.   Two weeks after the conversation, Bob's company ordered 500 metric tons of hot-rolled steel. Sarah's company delivered it, and Bob's company accepted it.

A.   The contract is only enforceable for 500 metric tons.

B.   The parties have a requirements contract for three months.

C.   The parties have an output contract for three months.

D.   A and B

92.   With respect to the steel that has been delivered and accepted in the preceding question, Bob's company must

A.   return it.

B.   negotiate in good faith to reach a price.

C.   pay $275 per metric ton.

D.   pay market price because no writing states the price.

93.   A signed agreement contains a clause that says, "This Agreement states the complete, final, and exclusive statement of all agreements of the parties, from the beginning of the world until the date hereof." No evidence is offered to contradict the clause. The agreement is

    A.   completely integrated.

    B.   partially integrated.

    C.   not integrated.

    D.   in pari materia.

94.   The agreement in the preceding question

    A.   may be supplemented by oral terms.

    B.   may be supplemented by consistent terms.

    C.   precludes the introduction of evidence of a modification.

    D.   none of the above.

95.   Which of the following is admissible with respect to the preceding agreement?

    A.   Evidence of earlier written agreements

    B.   Evidence of earlier oral agreements

    C.   Evidence of contemporaneous written agreements

    D.   Evidence of contemporaneous oral agreements

96. Which of the following is admissible with respect to the preceding agreement?

    A.   Evidence of lack of consideration

    B.   Evidence of failure of consideration

    C.   Evidence of fraud

    D.   All of the above

97. Buyer sends a purchase order to Seller, ordering 3000 cubic yards of play-grade sand for $25 per cubic yard. Seller responds with a confirmation that is identical to the purchase order on all terms (including price, delivery date, etc.), except it says that disputes will be settled by arbitration. Buyer receives the confirmation and does nothing. You may assume that sand is a good. If neither party has performed yet,

    A.   there is no contract because of the mirror image rule.

    B.   there is no contract because of the knockout rule.

    C.   there would perhaps be no contract at common law, but there is a contract in this case.

    D.   there is a contract if both parties are merchants.

98.   Use the same facts, but now suppose the sand has been delivered and paid for. One term of the contract is

A.   an implied warranty of fitness for a particular purpose.

B.   an implied warranty that the sand is play grade.

C.   an express warranty that the sand is play grade.

D.   A and C

99.   Molly writes a letter to her daughter, saying, "Cheryl, I want you to move back here from Boston. You're 2000 miles away, and I would like you to be closer to me as I grow older. As you know, I'm moving into a condo next month, and I'm going to deed my old house over to you. If you don't move here, I know you'll just want to sell it, which would be too bad. Why not move into it? This place is so nice for raising families." She signed at the bottom.

When Cheryl got the letter, she called her mother and agreed. They decided they would work out the details later. The next week, Cheryl wrote, "I'll move back in the spring. I want to finish off the year in my job here to make sure I get my bonus." She signed at the bottom.

The following week, Molly's son Sid, who had been estranged from his mother, made everything up with her. He convinced his mother not to give the house to Cheryl. Molly immediately sent her daughter a letter with the good news (making up with Sid) and bad news (Cheryl could not have the house anymore). It is now October. If Cheryl wants to enforce the agreement, you would advise her that she

A.   has a contract. She and her mother had reached an agreement, which constitutes mutual assent.

B.   has a contract. She and her mother were mutually inducing each other.

C.   does not have a contract, as there is no consideration.

D.   has a contract for the reasons in A and B.

100. In the preceding question, you would advise your client that she

A.   can probably enforce the agreement under a promissory estoppel theory.

B.   can probably enforce the agreement as a contract.

C.   cannot enforce the contract under a theory of promissory estoppel.

D.   A and B

CONTRACTS
MULTIPLE CHOICE

ANSWERS &
ANALYSIS

CONTRACTS ANSWERS AND ANALYSIS

1. **Issue: Limitations on damages.**
    Answer: C, This measure of damages reflects the effect of her so-called "duty" to mitigate.

2. **Issue: Limitations on damages.**
    Answer: B. It is commonly said that the aggrieved party has a duty to mitigate damages, so "A" is a tempting choice. But the only effect of that "duty" is that he will be treated as if he had made reasonable efforts to mitigate. So Paul will be awarded damages as if he had tried to resell the skis to someone else, even if he doesn't do so.

3. **Issue: Limitations on damages**
    Answer: D. If it's not too hard to sell skis right now, and since Paul will be treated as if he had tried to resell, and given that he's likely to get $200 for them, he has close to no damages.

4. **Issue: Statute of Frauds**
    Answer: D. This contract, for a price well under $500, does not need to be in writing under the statute of frauds. See UCC § 2-201.

5. **Issue: Measure of damages**
    Answer: A. Darlene has received nothing at this point, so there is no benefit for her to disgorge, and no unjust enrichment of Darlene.

6. **Issue: Measure of damages**
    Answer: B. Paula has incurred $20 in expenses. By awarding her $20, she will be put where she would be had there been no contract.

7. **Issue: Expectation damages**
    Answer: D. Paula won't be able to resell this blanket because it is customized for Darlene's baby.

She should therefore be able to recover the whole price. See UCC § 2-709(1)(b).

8.   **Issue: Specific performance**
      Answer: A. Although specific performance would be appropriate in a case like B, the concept in A is a better statement of the test for specific performance in goods cases because the goods need not be truly unique. See UCC § 2-716 & cmt. 2.

9.   **Issue: Specific performance**
      Answer: A. Land has traditionally been presumed to be unique. Courts traditionally have not liked to supervise construction and have not wanted to infringe liberty by ordering specific performance in a personal services contract. Most goods can generally be obtained from other sellers, so there is no need for specific performance.

10.   **Issue: Offer and acceptance**
      Answer: A. Courts are reluctant to interpret parties into a binding agreement (i.e., a contract), but are willing to do more interpretation to save an agreement that was intended to be a binding contract.

11.   **Issue: Cancellation**
      Answer: B. This is a cancellation because the contract is being ended because of Bob's breach.

12.   **Issue: Cancellation**
      Answer: C. The UCC provides that any right based on prior breach or performance survives.

13.   **Issue: Termination**
      Answer: A. The contract has not been breached, so it is terminated, not cancelled. The cancellation cannot take effect for 10 days according to the terms of the contract.

14. **Issue: Termination**
Answer: B. This is a claim based on a breach
before termination, although the termination is not
based on the breach..

15. **Issue: Offer and acceptance**
Answer: B. Catalogs, which are circulated to many
people, are rarely offers. They are generally
invitations to receive offers. The buyer's order was
an offer.

16. **Issue: Offer and acceptance**
Answer: C. Buyer offered to buy by making the
order. Seller accepted by shipping the goods, which
is a performance. Acceptance by performance
forms a unilateral contract.

17. **Issue: Assignability**
Answer: A. Rights are assigned; duties are
delegated. Contract rights may generally be
assigned unless the contract says otherwise.

18. **Issue: Delegation**
Answer: C. Absent a novation, both the delegor
and delegate remain liable, since the other party
never agreed to a contract with the delegate. Duties
under personal services contracts may not be
delegated since those contracts are of a personal
nature, and the identity of the performing party
matters.

19. **Issue: Contractual limitation of remedy**
Answer: B. B is the best answer pursuant to UCC
§§ 2-715 cmt. 3 and 2-719. Note, though, that
disclaimer of consequential damages for personal
injury is prima facie unconscionable in a case
involving consumer goods under UCC §2-719(3).

20. **Issue: Measure of damages**
Answer: C. Since plaintiff has himself materially

breached, he can generally only collect ("off the contract") the amount by which he has unjustly enriched the defendant (the non-breaching party). Note that if expectancy is lower than restitution, expectancy will be the measure of damages, but that would be an exceptional situation. Hence C, not A, is the best answer. The question is based on Britton v. Turner.

21.   **Issue: Contract enforceability**
Answer: A. There appears to be no bargained-for exchange. The employee is not getting any promise or performance. Thus the lack of consideration prevents the arbitration clause from being binding, according to some decisions (although other decisions disagree). In any event, the other alternatives—B, C, and D—are all incorrect. There is a policy in favor of arbitration. Parol evidence has nothing to do with this issue. The application is written, so the statute of frauds presents no obstacle.

22.   **Issue: Option contracts**
Answer: C. This is a modern equivalent of the famous case of Dickinson v. Dodds. Offers can be revoked at any time unless there is consideration, promissory estoppel, or some applicable exception—none of which is present here.

23.   **Issue: Bases of recovery**
Answer: D. This question is based on the famous case of Hawkins v. McGee and the related insurance coverage litigation, although it changes some of the facts. The negligence gives rise to the tort action. The express guarantee, especially in the context of his having sought to do the surgery, gives rise to an express contract. And even though nothing is said about the matter, there is generally an implied contract for the physician to use

ordinary care and for the patient to pay.

24. **Issue: Bases of recovery**
Answer: C. While "tort" could possibly be a better answer, it is not a choice. Based on the circumstances, there is generally an implied contract for the patient to pay and for the physician to use reasonable care. Rarely do physicians make express promises (although they do sometimes, as when Dr. McGee promised Hawkins a 100% good hand). It is relatively unlikely that John would want to recover for having unjustly enriched the physician; he wants to recover for his own injuries.

25. **Issue: Contract enforceability**
Answer: D. The parties have reached an agreement, even though they have used informal words, so there is mutual assent (even if we cannot figure out exactly what is the offer and what is the acceptance). They have exchanged promises— promised labor for promised money; there is mutual inducement and a bargained-for exchange, i.e., consideration. Labor contracts that can be performed within a year are not required to be in writing under the statute of frauds, and since Hugh is to provide the materials, there is no problem of the statute of frauds for sales of goods of $500 or more.

26. **Issue: Contract modification**
Answer: A. There is no fresh consideration for this modification; Carl is not inducing Hugh to do anything by the $100-a-day promise. The pre-existing duty rule, though much criticized, is still part of the common law. It has been abolished by UCC § 2-209, but that only applies to transactions in goods. There is no statute of frauds requirement for this kind of agreement to be in writing. And it is no more binding as a side agreement than as a

modification.

27. **Issue: Expectation Damages**
Answer: D. Carl will presumably be liable for the usual expectancy damages.

28. **Issue: Limitations on damages**
Answer: D. Carl will be liable because he was informed at the time of contracting of the upcoming wedding, and this sort of expense becomes foreseeable once Carl is given notice of that special circumstance. There is no requirement that he agree expressly (as in A) to take on that liability. Without notice of the wedding, B or C might be correct, but he did have notice.

29. **Issue: Liquidated damages**
Answer: C. Liquidated damages are generally enforceable if they are reasonable in light of the anticipated harm, the difficulty of proving damages, and (in some formulations) the actual harm. This is true under the common law and the UCC. Damages that are actually a penalty are not valid, although some (like Posner) have suggested that perhaps they should be.

30. **Issue: Lost-volume seller**
Answer: B. A lost-volume seller is one who, but for the breach, would have had two sales and two profits. That will usually include dealers, but will not include someone with a limited supply of goods (as in C) or services (as in A). Ansel can easily fill his time with another subject to be painted. The friend can presumably sell his yacht to someone else for about the same price; also, there is no indication that Chester was going to pay the friend more than the market value of the yacht.

31. **Issue: Statute of frauds**
Answer: A. A new car will likely cost more than

$500 and is thus subject to the requirements of UCC § 2-201. A lease of an apartment for one year might be within the land or one-year provisions of the statute of frauds, but leases for one-year or less are generally excepted from the statute. The six-month loan does not fall within any of the provisions of the statute.

32. **Issue: Third-party beneficiaries**
Answer: A. These are the traditional classes recognized by the cases.

33. **Issue: Contract enforceability**
Answer: D. None of these involves the parties mutually inducing each other, so there is no bargained-for exchange. While B and C can lead to binding contracts in exceptional situations, they do not "ordinarily" do so, and D is the best answer.

34. **Issue: Disclaimer of warranty**
Answer: B. An "as is" disclaimer is expressly allowed by the Code in § 2-316(3)(a), so B is the best answer. There is some argument that all merchantability disclaimers should be written, but the Code does not say that, and A is not as good an answer as B. The warranty only attaches in sales of goods by a merchant who deals in goods of the kind, so C is not correct.

35. **Issue: Disclaimer of warranty**
Answer: A. For fitness disclaimers, the Code requires a writing and conspicuous disclaimer under § 2-316(2) (so A is correct—the fitness warranty can be so disclaimed). Fitness disclaimers—like all implied warranties—may also be disclaimed through "as is" or the like under § 2-316(3)(a) (so B is not correct). According to most authorities, the fitness warranty assures the buyer that that the goods are fit for the particular purpose—not the ordinary purpose, which is

covered by the merchantability warranty. Although there is some contrary argument on the last point, A is the best answer.

36. **Issue: Statute of frauds**
Answer: B is the best answer. Under the statute, the writing must be signed (so C is incorrect), and the contract is not enforceable beyond the quantity indicated (so A is probably incorrect). Quantity is more clearly required by the final paragraph of comment 1. Although there is an argument that the statutory text does not require quantity to be stated, it is quite clear that price need not be stated. Thus B is the best answer.

37. **Issue: Adequate assurances of performance**
Answer: C. Farmer has not unequivocally repudiated the contract, only saying that he "may not be able to deliver" by the contract date. Thus it is not an anticipatory repudiation, and if Buyer fails to pay on time, Buyer may be found in breach. Thus A and D are not the best answers. Telephoning the seller (as in B) is not in writing and does not preserve Buyer's rights. To do that, Buyer must request adequate assurances in writing under UCC § 2-609.

38. **Issue: Perfect tender**
Answer: D. In a single-delivery sale of goods, the perfect tender rule still applies (broadly speaking), see UCC § 2-601, and a delivery that is a week late is not a perfect tender. The substantial impairment test and material breach doctrines do not apply, so A, B, and C are incorrect. Also, A misstates the effect of the substantial impairment test.

39. **Issue: Substantial impairment/material breach**
Answer: A, in which case it is an installment contract and is subject to the substantial impairment test of UCC § 2-612 (much like the

common-law material breach test). Even with that test, however, the seller is still liable for damages; the effect of the substantial impairment test is not on damages but on keeping the contract in place (or not). B is irrelevant and thus incorrect.

40. **Issue: Cover damages**
Answer: C. Buyer may cover, but need not do so. See UCC § 2-712. Failing to cover, however, may result in damages that could have been avoided, and avoidable damages cannot be recovered from the seller. See id. § 2-715(2)(a).

41. **Issue: Cover damages**
Answer: A. As long as cover is commercially reasonable, buyer is entitled to cover price ($27,500) minus contract price ($25,000), plus incidentals (the brokerage commission, see UCC § 2-715(1)) and consequentials (none indicated). See UCC § 2-712(2). Covering within 48 hours of knowing the breach should be commercially reasonable, absent any facts to indicate otherwise, and covering a day earlier would not have helped. Therefore the court would not use the $270 market price on the date of delivery.

42. **Issue: Buyer's damages**
Answer: C. In the absence of cover, buyer gets the difference between the market price when the buyer learned of the breach (April 15, when the delivery did not happen, so $27,000) minus the contract price ($25,000), plus incidental and consequential damages (none indicated). See UCC § 2-713.

43. **Issue: Seller's damages**
Answer: C. Seller is entitled to the difference between the contract price ($25,000) and the market price at the time and place for tender ($20,000), plus incidental damages. See UCC § 2-708.

44. **Issue: Unilateral contract**
    Answer: B. The contract involved an exchange of a promise for a promise. It was not accepted by performance, so A is not correct. There is no indication that this is all of the farmer's grain (an output contract) or that it is all of the grain that the buyer needs or requires (a requirements contract).

45. **Issue: Parol evidence**
    Answer: D. A is allowed because the writing is only partially integrated. The parol evidence rule never excludes evidence of B or C.

46. **Issue: Scope of UCC Article 2**
    Answer: A. This is a transaction in goods, and Article 2 governs. See § 2-102.

47. **Issue: Statute of frauds**
    Answer: D. They have a contract, because there is mutual assent and consideration. That contract is not enforceable under the statute of frauds, UCC § 2-201. A and B are correct. The statute of frauds, although it makes the contract unenforceable, does not render the contract void, see id. cmt. 4, so C is not correct.

48. **Issue: Acceptance**
    Answer: D. An offer for prompt or current shipment may be accepted by a prompt promise or shipment, even if the shipped goods are nonconforming. See UCC § 2-206(1)(b).

49. **Issue: Merchant status**
    Answer: D. Although Best Bearings is not a merchant with respect to goods of the kind (it sells bearings, not furniture, so B is true), as a company in business it has knowledge of the practices involved here—making contracts. It is therefore a merchant, and A is right and C is wrong. See UCC

§ 2-104(1) and especially comment 2.

50. **Issue: Contract modification**
Answer: D. There is no consideration for the modification, so the modification is not enforceable under the pre-existing duty rule. A and B would be relevant only under UCC Article 2, which does not govern this transaction. Absent unconscionability or the like, courts do not look into adequacy of consideration.

51. **Issue: Third-party beneficiaries**
Answer: B. Darlene is a classic donee beneficiary, and is a clearly intended (as opposed to incidental) beneficiary of the contract; therefore, even though she is not a party to the contract, she can enforce it. Saul is essentially giving Darlene a donation. C would have been tempting if it said that Darlene "can" enforce the contract, as intended beneficiaries can do. Darlene was not a creditor of Saul's, so A is wrong.

52. **Issue: Assignment and delegation**
Answer: D. No duties were delegated to Darlene. She got the right to receive payments in the original contract; no rights were assigned afterwards. So none of the above is accurate.

53. **Issue: Effect of assignment**
Answer: A. Assignment of rights extinguishes the rights in the assignor. Only Gary holds the rights now. Otherwise, the other party (Betty) could be subjected to multiple and conflicting obligations, as here.

54. **Issue: Mutual inducement**
Answer: D. This is based on the famous case of <u>Ricketts v. Scothorn</u>, although the facts are changed a bit. While Saul's action may have resulted in Darlene's detrimental reliance, there is

no mutual inducement. The parties were not trying to induce the other's promise or action, so there is no bargained-for exchange, and no consideration. Moral consideration is not adequate. The moral obligation exception (encapsulated in § 86 of the Restatement (Second) of Contracts) does not apply, as Darlene has conferred no cognizable benefit on Saul.

55. **Issue: Promissory estoppel**
Answer: C. Rescission will do Darlene no good, since she wants to enforce the promise, not have it rescinded. A breach of contract action is not the best answer, as it usually presumes a contract based on consideration. Promissory estoppel is a better, more precise answer. Quasi-contract is not a good answer because Darlene has not unjustly enriched Saul.

56. **Issue: Measure of damages**
Answer: B. More modern cases, and orthodox modern doctrine, call for reliance damages to remedy the injustice occasioned in promissory estoppel cases. Many cases award expectancy, however. Restitution is not generally used, so A is wrong. Specific performance and other equitable relief are not appropriate for monetary promises. Thus B is the best answer.

57. **Issue: Formalities**
Answer: D. The power of the seal to make promises binding has been abolished in most jurisdictions.

58. **Issue: Limitations of remedies**
Answer: D. Under UCC § 2-719, limitation of remedies for commercial losses is not prima facie unconscionable, and courts rarely find unconscionability in commercial cases.

59. **Issue: Mutual assent**
     Answer: C is the best answer. Although contracts
     of adhesion—"take it or leave it"contracts—may be
     more likely to be unconscionable, they are still
     generally valid. The great run of consumer
     contracts are adhesionary (i.e., not subject to
     negotiation) but are perfectly valid; courts relatively
     rarely find contracts unconscionable. A is
     incorrect. Several relatively recent leading cases
     have held as indicated in C (such as <u>ProCD v.
     Zeidenberg</u> and <u>Hill v. Gateway 2000</u>), making B
     incorrect. Those cases currently represent the
     weight of judicial authority, despite a fair amount of
     academic outcry.

60. **Issue: Mistake**
     Answer: A. It is a belief not in accord with the
     facts. Answer B, C, and D involve beliefs about the
     future, not beliefs about facts.

61. **Issue: Reformation**
     Answer: A. Reformation requires a heightened
     standard of proof because otherwise the parol
     evidence rule would be undermined, since
     reformation allows a change to a written contract—
     even an integrated one.

62. **Issue: Frustration of purpose**
     Answer: A. Of the choices, the buyer only has to
     pay money, which (so far as the law is concerned) is
     not generally impracticable, but may be useless
     (because the purpose of the contract has been
     frustrated). All the others—seller, lessor, licensor—
     are more likely to plead impracticability, e.g.,
     because of inability to delivery on account of fire,
     act of God, and so on.

63. **Issue: Defenses**
     Answer: C. Infancy and incapacity lead to
     contracts voidable at the behest of the infant or

incapacitated person. With duress by force, there is no consent, and no contract at all.

64. **Issue: Anticipatory repudiation**
     Answer: D. This is an unequivocal statement by VSU that the contract will be performed. It is thus an anticipatory repudiation of the contract, which is a kind of breach of contract. A and B are correct. C is not correct. An unequivocal statement that the contract will not performed counts as a present breach, even if the time for performance has not yet arrived, and the promisee may immediately resort to remedies.

65. **Issue: Constructive conditions**
     Answer: D. Because of the agreed order of performance, Willa must do the work before Owen has an instant duty to pay. Until she does the work, he only has a conditional duty.

66. **Issue: Constructive conditions**
     Answer: A. Neither party has a duty to perform until the other does; they must perform at the same time. They are thus concurrent conditions. The hypo is based on the seminal case of <u>Morton v. Lamb</u>.

67. **Issue: Constructive conditions**
     Answer: D. Courts will not imply a condition in this situation, where the breach is minor and inadvertent, so it is not a constructive condition. <u>Jacob & Youngs v. Kent</u> so holds. The parties have not said that replacement by the contractor is a condition to the owner's duty to pay, so it is not an express condition. Replacement does not discharge the owner's duty to pay, so it is not a condition subsequent. Still, the contractor has said it would make these replacements, so it is a promise.

68. **Issue: Conditions**
    Answer: D. Because it is not a condition (see the explanation in the previous problem), the owner still has to pay, so A is correct and C is not. But because the contractor has breached the promise, it will have to pay any damages (making B correct also).

69. **Issue: Substantial performance**
    Answer: D. In cases of substantial performance, the courts prefer the difference in market value as the measure of damages rather than the cost of completion, especially where the cost of completion would appear to be wasteful, as here (because of having to tear down a significant part of the structure and because there is no difference in the quality of the fixtures). Cost of completion and market-value differential are different ways of putting the injured party where it would be had the contract been kept, so they are both forms of expectancy damages. Thus A and C are correct, making D the right answer.

70. **Issue: Contract interpretation**
    Answer: D. Is it established in the industry or by the parties' practice that variations of, say, 10% are allowable? If so, their agreement is interpreted in the light of that custom or practice. See UCC § 1-201(3) (which is 1-201(b)(3) in the revision); see also § 2-207 cmt. 4 (leeway allowed by custom). Until you know what their "agreement" calls for, you cannot reach the conclusions stated in A or B. C is untrue. Also note that this appears to be a single-delivery contract, so the substantial impairment test in B does not apply.

71. **Issue: Perfect tender**
    Answer: A. Because this is not an installment contract, the buyer may reject the delivery if the goods "fail in any respect to conform to the

contract." UCC § 2-601. This is the perfect tender rule. The substantial impairment test (in B and C, and implicated in D) does not apply to this contract.

72. **Issue: Right to cure**
Answer: C. Although the UCC keeps the perfect tender rule, it tempers its effects with the right to cure in certain circumstances. See § 2-508.

73. **Issue: Good faith**
Answer: B. The Code imposes an obligation of good faith, which at least for merchants includes both honesty in fact and observance of reasonable commercial standards of fair dealing. B is thus the best answer. The second prong of this test is about objective fairness, not reasonableness, and there is no applicable duty to be reasonable anyway. Thus A is not the best answer. Usage of trade will be displaced by the express provisions of this contract, so C is not promising. There is no Article 2 gap filler fitting the description in D that would help for this contract. The closest would be the provision on output and requirements contracts, which does not apply here. Note that B will not necessarily win for the seller on these facts, but it is the most promising of the choices given.

74. **Issue: Contract formation**
Answer: A. Consideration need not have passed for the contract to be enforceable, so B is wrong. Reliance is not an element for contract formation and is irrelevant here, so C is wrong. This contract need not be in writing under the statute of frauds, so D is wrong.

75. **Issue: Contract formation**
Answer: D. As Wonell and Tuel made a contract, there is no longer a revocable offer—they have a contract—so A is wrong, as is B. There is no legal

obstacle to Tuel making a contract with Tom, even though it appears that Tuel will not be able to perform, so C is wrong. Tuel has reached agreements with both Wonell and Tom, and those agreements are supported by consideration because the parties exchanged mutually induced promises. D is therefore correct.

76. **Issue: Scope of the UCC**
Answer: D. This is a transaction in goods and is therefore governed by Article 2. All transactions governed by the UCC are also governed by the general provisions in Article 1. A and B are thus correct, making D the right answer. This is true regardless of whether the parties are merchants, so C is wrong.

77. **Issue: Contract construction**
Answer: A. The whole reason for the default rules or gap fillers is to fill in the gaps of the parties' agreement. Even though they did not initially agree about delivery, the default rule fills the gap. Under the default rule, delivery is at the seller's place, so John had to pick it up, and A is correct. Since the gap is filled, there is no uncertainty, and D is not correct. Merchant status is irrelevant on this particular point, eliminating B and C.

78. **Issue: Contract modification**
Answer: B. "A" would be correct at common law, but UCC § 2-209 abolishes that rule for transactions in goods. This appears to be a good faith modification and thus unobjectionable under the UCC. Reliance, as in C and D, are irrelevant.

79. **Issue: Restitution**
Answer: A. Restitution looks to benefits conferred on the promisor (John). He has received no benefit to disgorge, so restitution is zero.

80.   **Issue: Resale damages**
Answer: A. Put in terms of the UCC formula, seller is entitled to contract price minus the resale, plus incidental damages, minus costs avoided. The contract price is $400, minus the $400 resale price, which leads to zero damages. There were no incidental damages or costs avoided. As it turned out, Claire is exactly where she would have been had John kept the (modified) contract. She did take the cab, but she was obligated to do that anyway under the modified contract, so she is no worse off.

81.   **Issue: Limitations on damages**
Answer: C. It was probably not foreseeable to the railroad that the plant would be closed because of this problem, so A and B are not recoverable damages. This is simply a modern variation of Hadley v. Baxendale. It is entirely foreseeable to the railroad that if it delays delivery for two weeks, then the plant will lose the use of the masticator for that period. This loss of use is probably easiest measured by what it would cost to rent one. C is thus the correct answer, making D necessarily incorrect.

82.   **Issue: Limitations on damages**
Answer: C. Profits for established businesses can usually be proved with reasonable certainty (even though profits might be too speculative for some new businesses, or one-time sporting or entertainment events). Thus A and B are wrong. The railroad probably could not foresee that the absence of the masticator would shut down the OCP plant. How would the railroad know? In any event, so holds Hadley v. Baxendale, and it has been followed on this point by modern courts. D is not really relevant on these facts, and as the answer is phrased, would not be helpful to

defendant anyway.

83. **Issue: Reliance damages**
Answer: B. If it is not clear whether your client would have made a profit, then you will not be able to prove a positive expectancy with reasonable certainty, so you would prefer to recover all $400,000 in reliance costs. A is not true because if you could prove that it was a great bargain for your client, you would prefer to recover expectancy, including both the $400,000 and the big profits. It is hard to tell what the effect of C would be, and while perhaps not irrelevant, it is not as good an answer as B. If your client were well financed, it might be more tempting to try even for unclear expectancy, hiring fancy experts, so D is not the best answer.

84. **Issue: Burden of proving damages with certainty**
Answer: D. Plaintiff may sue for reliance damages (so A is wrong). The party in breach, when Plaintiff sues for reliance, then can try to reduce reliance by showing that expectancy is lower. It is true that expectancy is the cap on damages (so C is wrong), but expectancy is uncertain (see the preceding question), which makes D correct and B inapplicable.

85. **Issue: Mutual assent**
Answer: D. The name of the ship is objectively ambiguous, and the parties subjectively have not agreed. There is no agreement on the same thing, and thus no contract. There are no facts to support an interpretation along the lines of A or B, and without knowing which ship is involved, there is no way to order specific performance (C). D is the holding of the famous PEERLESS case, <u>Raffles v. Wichelhaus</u>, and is the best answer.

86. **Issue: Unilateral contract formation**

Answer: D. The firm's offer required her to start work, and that is what she did. She accepted by performance, forming a unilateral contract. To perform, she had to start work in Chicago, so the employment contract was not formed until then (i.e., in Illinois).

87. **Issue: Option contract**

Answer: D. When the offer requires acceptance by performance, as this offer did, an option contract is formed when the offeree (Lynn) begins performance. See Restatement (Second) of Contracts § 45. Part of what was stipulated in the offer was quitting her job and going to Chicago, so it seems fair to characterize those activities as performance rather than mere preparation, especially given the reliance costs to Lynn. Cf. White v. Corlies & Tifft. Thus A and B are not the best answers under modern law. Cf. Petterson v. Pattberg. Once she quit her job and started going to Chicago, the option contract was formed under § 45 (and the offer became irrevocable.) Thus D is correct. Until she began what the offer requested, however, the offer could be revoked (making C incorrect). This hypothetical is based on a modern case, Petersen v. Ray-Hof Agencies.

88. **Issue: Unilateral contract formation**

Answer: C. The employment contract was not formed until she completed performance, as explained above. What prevents the offer from being revoked is the option contract that courts find when an offeree must incur reliance costs in beginning performance of a unilateral contract. While B is generally true, modern courts do not follow it on these facts. This is a unilateral contract situation, so D is wrong.

89. **Issue: Certainty**
    Answer: D. There is mutual assent, and there is consideration, so they would have a contract except that they have not agreed on a quantity. A court could not fix a remedy for a breach, so the agreement is not legally enforceable and is thus not a contract (so A is wrong). The parol evidence rule is irrelevant, so B is wrong. The statute of frauds does not prevent contract formation under UCC § 2-201, so C is wrong.

90. **Issue: Certainty**
    Answer: A. The certainty problem has been solved by Bob's commitment to get all the hot-rolled steel that his company requires from Sarah's company. Especially with the minimum, the quantity is now sufficiently certain, especially in light of the obligation of good faith. See UCC § 2-306. D is therefore wrong and A is right. This is not a contract calling for as much hot-rolled steel as Sarah's company can produce, so it is not an output contract. C is wrong for the reasons stated above.

91. **Issue: Statute of frauds**
    Answer: D. B is correct for the reasons stated above, including the three-month term to which the parties agreed. "A" is also correct because this contract, involving the sale of goods for well over $500, must be written to be enforceable, although part performance saves the 500 tons. See UCC § 2-201. C is wrong for the reasons stated above.

92. **Issue: Statute of frauds**
    Answer: C. As to the steel that has been delivered and accepted, there is an enforceable contract under the part performance exception. As Bob's company has accepted the steel, it must pay the contract price.

93.   **Issue: Integration**
Answer: A. The merger clause says there are no
other agreements outside the writing, so they are all
merged into the writing, which is thus completely
integrated (making A correct and B and C wrong).
The answer in D, which states a rule of
construction, is irrelevant.

94.   **Issue: Parol evidence**
Answer: D. Given its complete integration,
evidence of A and B are inadmissible. The parol
evidence rule does not exclude evidence of
modifications, which necessarily come after the
writing was executed.

95.   **Issue: Parol evidence**
Answer: C. The parol evidence rule excludes
evidence of all prior agreements (A and B) and
contemporaneous oral agreements (D), but not
contemporaneous written agreements.

96.   **Issue: Parol evidence**
Answer: D. The parol evidence rule always allows
evidence of invalidating cause, which includes
everything listed.

97.   **Issue: Acceptance**
Answer: C. There would be no contract under the
common-law mirror image rule, but there is a
contract in this case because the UCC abolishes
that rule (making A incorrect). See § 2-207(1), or in
the revision, § 2-206(3). The addition of the
arbitration clause thus does not defeat contract
formation, so C is correct. B is wrong; it refers to a
rule under the old § 2-207, and that rule does not
prevent contract formation. Merchant status is
also irrelevant to contract formation (although it
can be relevant to what terms are part of the
contract). Thus D is incorrect.

98. **Issue: Express warranties**
    Answer: C. The seller's form says it is to be play-grade sand. This is an express warranty: it is a promise or affirmation relating to the goods that is part of the basis of the bargain. See UCC § 2-313. As the parties have stipulated this quality in so many words, it is hardly an implied warranty, making B wrong. There are no facts to make us think the fitness warranty would attach; nothing indicates that seller even knows buyer's particular purpose. See § 2-315. A and D are therefore incorrect.

99. **Issue: Mutual inducement**
    Answer: C. Molly's initial letter says that she is going to give Cheryl the house, and the gift is not contingent on Cheryl moving in. In fact, the letter says that Cheryl might sell the house. Molly therefore is not promising to give the house in exchange for Cheryl's promise to move back. Without such inducement, there is no consideration, and the agreement is not enforceable. B is therefore wrong. Agreement alone is insufficient to form a contract, so A is wrong.

100. **Issue: Promissory estoppel**
    Answer: C. Cheryl has not relied on Molly's promise, so promissory estoppel will not work, and C is the best answer. This makes A wrong. B is wrong for the reasons given above.